Polyphemus and Galatea

FOR RODOLFO AND
ELECTRA CARDONA

« Aquélla soy, sin quien no hay felicidad en el mundo y
con quien toda infelicidad se pasa. En las demás
dichas de la vida se hallan muy divididas las ventajas
del bien, pero en mí todas concurren, la honra, el
gusto y el provecho. »
« Ahora digo que eres la Amistad . . . »

Gracián

LUIS DE GÓNGORA

Polyphemus and Galatea

A STUDY IN THE
INTERPRETATION
OF A
BAROQUE
POEM

ALEXANDER A. PARKER

with verse translation by
GILBERT F. CUNNINGHAM

University of Texas Press
AUSTIN
1977

International Standard Book Number 0-292-72421-7
Library of Congress Catalog Card Number 77-81914
Copyright © 1977 by Edinburgh University Press
Printed in Great Britain by
W & J Mackay Limited
Chatham

Preface

WHEN I MOVED TO Edinburgh University in 1963 I had the privilege of meeting Gilbert Cunningham. Our acquaintance quickly grew into a friendship marked by admiration on my part for his interest in literature and his remarkable gifts as a translator. He had then completed the translation of Góngora's *Soledades*, which was later (1968) published by the Johns Hopkins Press. I myself felt in 1963 that the cause of attracting English-speaking readers to Góngora's poetry would be better served by publishing first a translation of the shorter, more closely-wrought and thematically more accessible *Polifemo*, especially since there already existed Professor Edward M. Wilson's fine translation of *Soledades* (Minority Press, Cambridge 1931; reprinted C.U.P. 1965).

Cunningham readily accepted my suggestion that he should defer publication of his *Solitudes* until after he could complete and publish a translation of *Polifemo*. This was finished in 1965, and the Edinburgh University Press accepted it for its Bilingual Library, a new series that was then being planned. I offered to write the Introduction and Notes. Meanwhile, the Press gave Cunningham permission to issue a private limited edition for presentation to his friends at Christmas of that year.

His untimely death less than two years later postponed the preparation of the volume for the Bilingual Library. The private edition had carried as Introduction a short interpretation of the poem by me, and the intention had been to amplify that introduction and to annotate the text. The appearance, however, of Don Dámaso Alonso's masterly edition and exhaustive commentary, which rapidly went through several editions, made me reluctant to produce a volume that would inevitably rely very heavily on his. I therefore planned, instead, a study of Góngora's poem based on an approach that had not yet been systematically attempted—a study of Góngora's imagery as an example of

(v)

conceptismo, or Wit. Ever since his revaluation in the 1920s Góngora had been presented either as an exponent of 'pure poetry', or as a *culterano* with a heavily Latinized poetic style. It was clear to me that, despite his meticulous concern with form and the sensuous elaboration of his images, there was an all-pervading intellectual preoccupation which was characteristic of his age, and which made the concept of 'pure poetry' inapplicable to him; that, in other words, most of his images are conceits and not just poetic ornaments. Not being ready, at that time, to develop this particular approach, nor having the immediate leisure to embark on it, I shelved the project, with the result that it has taken much longer to complete than it ought to have done.

The justification for this new edition of *Polifemo*, therefore, is first to give Gilbert Cunningham's remarkable translation the wider diffusion it deserves, and secondly to present an interpretation of Góngora's poetry that, it is hoped, may have some novelty. His standing as a leading exponent of the 'Baroque' is universally accepted, but there is little constructive agreement on the definition of that term. In particular, while there is something near to consensus on the nature of 'metaphysical poetry' as regards English literature, there is little agreement on the wider definitions of Wit or the Conceit. To associate Góngora with the Spanish manifestation of this aspect of the Baroque is necessarily to associate him with Baltasar Gracián, whose *Agudeza y arte de ingenio* is a monumental analysis of Wit in all its forms. This is a sadly neglected work, but understandably so, for its unfamiliar terminology appears abstruse, its distinctions too subtle to be readily comprehensible, the organization of the material seems unsystematic and the arguments excessively involved. In short, it is too 'baroque' in the least engaging sense of the word.

Góngora was Gracián's favourite Spanish poet; he is quoted and discussed in *Agudeza* more than any other. By analysing much of the imagery of *Polifemo* in the light of Gracián's definitions— or, conversely, by illustrating these definitions from Góngora—I hope that this new study of his poem may perhaps help to restore Góngora more fully to his age than has hitherto been done, without thereby lessening the appeal he already has in ours. I also hope it may show that Gracián's *Agudeza*, while difficult, is not unintelligible, thereby supporting by direct analysis the attempts

(vi)

made by Edward Sarmiento and T. E. May, over forty and thirty
years ago respectively, to make him more accessible to the
general student of literature. But while I would hope that the
conceptismo of *Polifemo* has been adequately covered, it must be
emphasized that this volume does little more than touch the
surface of Gracián's treatise.

There seems to be a tendency nowadays to assume that if a
critic writes sympathetically of a writer of the past he is thereby
voicing his own opinions on literature and life, and so doing
propaganda for them. Criticism, like literature itself, must in the
view of many be 'committed'. Against such a view I would claim
that comprehension of a writer within his historical context is the
critic's main task, and that comprehension necessitates as much
sympathy and approval as possible, with a 'suspension of dis-
belief' where this is necessary; but I do not hold that sympathy
means identification, or that approval implies extension beyond
the historical context. If I try to make Gracián sound intelligent
and 'true', it is not because I think his particular 'art of the mind'
is necessarily valid for today. I do indeed maintain that his
Agudeza is extremely helpful for understanding seventeenth-
century poetry, but not necessarily the poetry of any other
century. Góngora's greatness as a poet is independent of time, but
his conception of poetry and his technique are of his age, not of
ours. His age does not deserve condemnation for being so different
from ours, any more than our age deserves unqualified approval
for being what it is.

Cunningham's private edition of his *Polyphemus* was published
with the Spanish text. He obtained permission from Don Dámaso
Alonso, now President of the Spanish Royal Academy, to repro-
duce his text from *Góngora y el Polifemo*, and he expressed his
thanks in his Preface as well as his acknowledgement of the
enormous help this learned study had been to him. Later, Don
Dámaso also gave me permission to reproduce his text, for which
I too would express my deep appreciation. I have faithfully
followed it with the exception of one change of punctuation
which I mention in my Notes. All textual variants and problems
are fully discussed in Don Dámaso's edition, and consequently no
mention is made of them here. Quite apart from the text my
indebtedness to Don Dámaso's scholarship and to his sensitive

criticism is incalculable. No one can write on *Polifemo*, or indeed on Góngora, without incurring a debt that no acknowledgement can repay.

A further debt of gratitude is owed by every student of *Polifemo* to Antonio Vilanova, whose two massive and erudite volumes on *Las fuentes y los temas del Polifemo de Góngora* collect countless parallels for his images and even for most of his phrases in Latin, Italian and Spanish literatures. This work is eloquent testimony to the extent to which Góngora, like all learned poets of his age, was steeped in the Latin classics.

Cunningham's private edition of his *Polyphemus* had as Appendix his own translation of the section from Ovid's *Metamorphoses* that was Góngora's source for the fable. This he composed in heroic couplets, which gave Ovid a rather formal and old-fashioned dress. The *ottava rima* of Cunningham's *Polyphemus* is not exactly modern, but it is Góngora's stanza; whereas the heroic couplet is farther removed from the tone of Ovid. I asked Mr David West, now Professor at the University of Newcastle upon Tyne, who made this objection, to write another translation. This is included in this present edition, with comments of his on the Ovid passage, and I would express my gratitude to him for his kind willingness to collaborate.

Cunningham made another acknowledgement as follows. 'Professor A.J.Steele has for some years now taken a keen and helpful interest in all my projects of translation. I am glad to have another opportunity of expressing my gratitude for his friendly co-operation.' This acknowledgement I also endorse. Professor Steele was associated, as guide and friend, with this *Polifemo* project from its commencement; his encouragement was instrumental in its getting under way and his advice has always been generously forthcoming.

Lastly, Cunningham thanked the Edinburgh University Press and its Secretary, Archie Turnbull, for having undertaken to publish his translation. For my part I must thank Mr Turnbull for his patience in waiting so long.

A.A.P.

Department of Spanish and Portuguese
University of Texas at Austin
November
1976

Contents

I

Foreword on the
Translation and the Translator

GILBERT CUNNINGHAM BEGAN the Preface to his private edition of *Polyphemus* with this paragraph.

Four years ago [1961], when I began the translation of Góngora's *Solitudes*, I still felt some doubt as to the author's poetic stature, and wondered indeed how far the labour involved might be justified. Long before I reached the end of the poem, however, I was conscious of splendours and excellences which my previous casual acquaintance had failed to discover. When Professor A.A.Parker, head of the Department of Hispanic Studies in the University of Edinburgh, suggested that I would find still greater pleasure, at the cost of even more arduous effort, in making an English version of the *Polifemo*, I embarked on the task with alacrity and enthusiasm. I quickly realised that I was dealing with what, as he says in his Introduction, is a masterpiece of world literature. To translate a poem which combines all the features which he enumerates in the succeeding pages is, of course, a forlorn hope at best, but I trust that I may have caught sufficient of its magic in the occasional happy phrase or well-turned stanza to attract the reader towards the Spanish on the opposite page, for there alone can he realise to the full the attractions which Góngora has to offer.

'Happy phrases' and 'well-turned stanzas' do indeed abound. One is struck immediately by the way the translation succeeds not only in rendering the sense but in reproducing so much of the formal structure of the Spanish lines, especially the bipartite balance so frequent at the close of Góngora's stanzas; where noun+ verb, or noun+ adjective, etc., are repeated in each part: 'A whistle gathers and a boulder locks' (48); 'The primal candour of a purer breed' (88). Cunningham keeps to this symmetrical phrasing when he changes the parts of speech, as for instance in: 'gimiendo tristes y volando graves' (40) [With ponderous wings and melancholy cries]. Especially skilful is a case like this, where there is rendering of the sense and symmetry without any verbal equivalent: 'mas discursiva y menos alterada' (232) [To ease her terrors and to soothe her mind].

Cunningham can also make the formal Gongorine construction, which Alonso has called 'A, if not B', sound quite natural:

> Uncertain folds of empty draperies
> Spread by Favonius' gentle breath, supplied
> A bed, if not a wind-swung hammock, made
> From slender couch-grass and refreshing shade. (213–16)

The rendering of *cama de viento* ('bed of wind'=hammock) as 'wind-swung hammock' could not be more felicitous. Even Góngora's complicated constructions are given in English a sufficiently complex rendering to convey the feel of the original:

> tantos jazmines cuanta hierba esconde
> la nieve de sus miembros ... (180)
> [Her snowy limbs no fewer scattering
> Of jasmines than they hide of greenery.]

As for well-turned stanzas, perhaps this one might be selected to show how closely Cunningham can capture the lyrical tenderness of these particular lines, and even, as far as English can, much of their lovely music:

> Fair maiden, gentler than a flower bent low
> When dawn's first dewdrop on its petals lies,
> With plumage whiter than the swan can show,
> Who dwells upon the sea, and singing dies,
> Splendid as is the peacock, for although
> His azure mantle shines with golden eyes
> Thick as the stars that stud the sapphire zone,
> No two are lovelier, maiden, than your own. (361–8)

Given the *ottava rima* and the 'Miltonic' language, *Polyphemus*, will doubtless sound Victorian to some ears. This was inevitable. It is compensated for by an astonishing fidelity to the sense of the original, which not so long ago used to be thought so obscure as to be almost incomprehensible.

There were some inaccuracies that I have ventured to remove

when I could do so without detriment to the rhythm, and occasionally I thought another word would be an improvement. I list here the changes I have made, italicizing the deleted word and giving the replacement in brackets.

  5 Hear, *if* Niebla's cloud you gild with light,   (since)
 79 Pale guardians these, who *jealously* withhold   (miserly)
 95 Fear wings with sail or oar the *fleeing* boats: (deafened)
112 Trinket in gold, hung from her *pearly* ear.   (shell-like)
238 The little blindfold love-god *longed* to take   (wills)
259 Kind to his sleep, but *cruelly* unaware   (blindly)
270 Despite the *shadowy* branches, she could see   (shading)
     The sketch which, like a *pencil*, Cupid's dart (paint brush)
281 The serpent lurks where some *unmown* expanse   (unshorn)
328 The *crystals flee*, the apples turn to snow   (crystal flees)
370 Of *Thetis'* daughters, and the waves shall learn   (Tethys)
     Though lit not by a car of golden fire   (when)
422 *As* in the sky a single eye *we see*:   (when, was seen)

Where the reason for a change I make might not be apparent, the explanation is given in the notes.

GILBERT FARM CUNNINGHAM was born in 1900 at Alva, Clackmannanshire. His father had founded in 1899 a printing firm in that small Scottish country town. This subsequently became Robert Cunningham and Sons, Ltd., when Gilbert and his brother joined it. Under Gilbert as Chairman and Managing Director it rose to the position of one of the leading firms of quality printing in Scotland. Shortly before his death it merged with the firm of R. and R. Clark of Edinburgh.

Cunningham laid the foundation of his abiding interest in literature at University College, London, where he graduated with a BA degree in English and where, as he was proud to recall, he was taught by W. P. Ker. In 1954 he was awarded the degree of PhD by Edinburgh University for a dissertation on the English translations of the *Divina Commedia*. This was subsequently expanded into a two-volume work and published by Oliver & Boyd. He remained devoted to the University, with some of whose members he formed close friendships. He took a special interest in the Press, to which he was always glad to render assistance whenever he could.

His literary interests centred in the art of translating poetry, which he pursued with remarkable versatility as a relaxation from his professional work as a printer. Printing for him was an art, not a trade, and the combination of professional activity at this level and a scholarly love of poetry made us who knew him recall the scholar-printers of the Renaissance. None-the-less, he remained quite unassuming, never losing the forthrightness, the kindly warmth and the rugged simplicity of a countryman. He loved nothing more than to take long walks over his native Ochil hills, and he composed his verse translations as he walked; the most intractable problems (he used to relate) solved themselves most easily in the open air.

Despite his skill as a translator Cunningham was not a linguist in the ordinary sense of the word. He could not really speak or write well, much less pronounce, any of the five modern languages he translated. Yet he had an instinct for languages, seen in his extraordinary flair for grasping, seemingly intuitively, the meaning of any passage of verse in these five. His first and always his principal love was Italian, but he translated also from Latin, French, German and Russian, turning last of all to Spanish near the end of his life. Without any previous formal instruction in that language he went straight to the difficult Góngora, and after completing his *Solitudes* and *Polyphemus*, he accepted the equally difficult challenge I put to him—the *Sueño* of the seventeenth-century Mexican poetess, Sor Juana Inés de la Cruz. The fragments which he showed me of this translation were as remarkable as anything he had previously done, and when I passed them on to Professor Elias Rivers, who had recently published a study of that extraordinary poem, he persuaded the Johns Hopkins Press to commission the complete translation. In the event Cunningham did not live to complete it or to see the publication of his *Solitudes*. He died on 25 August 1967.

The following is the list of his published books:

Translations from Goethe (Edinburgh 1949).
Poems by Eduard Mörike (London 1959) with some translations by Norah K. Cruikshank.
Lyrics from the Russian. With Biographical Notes by Militsa Greene. (Printed for private circulation, Alva 1961).
Jean de Sponde. Poems of Love and Death. (Edinburgh 1964).

The Divine Comedy in English: A Critical Bibliography.
Vol. I, 1782–1900 (Edinburgh 1965). Vol. II, 1901–66
(Edinburgh 1966).
Luis de Góngora y Argote. Polyphemus. With the Spanish text
and an Introduction by Alexander A. Parker
(Printed Privately, Alva 1965).
The Solitudes of Luis de Góngora. The Spanish text with an
English translation. Preface by A. A. Parker. Introduction by
Elias L. Rivers (Baltimore 1968).

II

Introduction

1. *The Mythological Fable*

The Cyclopes, one-eyed giants who were shepherds living in caverns, are connected with the Olympian myth of Creation. The story of the cyclops Polyphemus belongs, properly speaking, not to Myth but to Fable. How Ulysses strays into his cavern and finally escapes by driving a stake into his eye, and how he is pursued by the anger of Poseidon, father of the cyclops, is told in the *Odyssey*. The other aspect of the Polyphemus fable, his unsuccessful wooing of the nymph Galatea, was a favourite for centuries with poets—Theocritus, Bion, Virgil and Ovid among the ancients; Góngora the most prominent among the many moderns.

The attempt of the Stoics to interpret the pagan gods as symbols of the physical world, and to see the myths and fables as allegories conveying moral lessons, enabled these ancient stories to survive the coming of Christianity and to endure through the Middle Ages into the seventeenth century. While the Renaissance did not forget allegory or moralization, much less symbolism, it did restore the gods to their original form and allowed them to permeate the literature and art of the sixteenth century. The common store of mythological tales could serve to give dignity to the sensuous by endowing it with the sanction of antiquity and a certain, if remote, aura of the 'divine'. Intimately connected in painting, poetry and drama with the newly revived pastoralism and its wistful backward glance to the Golden Age of man's beginnings, mythology could also give plastic form to a nostalgia for beauty and innocence within a still uncorrupted nature.

This is what the background to the fable of Polyphemus, Acis and Galatea meant to Góngora, and to his predecessors and contemporaries. Stigmatized until fifty years ago as a typical example of the extravagances of the Baroque Age, the *Polifemo* is now universally acknowledged to be a poetic masterpiece of a period whose art is no longer scorned. It is a baroque poem *par excellence*, showing to a highly developed degree the characteristics of that style; 'Gongorism' has long been a synonym for baroque.

2. *The Baroque Styles*

Attempts to define a baroque style have proved unsuccessful.[1] Several elements have been separated, but no single one is universally valid for the literatures of all western Europe, and none is exclusively confined to the period in question. Definition, if it means the search for precision through exclusion, is perhaps impossible with the complex literature of a complex age; yet the need for it will always be felt. Góngora's 'elevated style', exemplified by *Polifemo* and *Las soledades*, has an obvious and remarkable unity, but the unity is artistic and not a necessary characteristic of the style. None of its distinctive features—lexical, syntactical, metaphorical, alliterative, prosodial—are such as to demand association together, and nearly all of them can be found in earlier literature. Yet *Polifemo* is essentially of its period: it could not have been written a century earlier or a century later. What was novel about 'Gongorism' in 1613 was precisely the association and unification of stylistic devices previously distinct. The unification is peculiar to Góngora: each of the other major baroque writers of Spain has a style that employs one or more of these devices, but not all of them together. There is, therefore, no single baroque style in Spain.

Outside Spain the simplest classification is one that recognizes three basic styles: 'Préciosité', an elegant, affectedly erudite, upper-class style; 'Metaphysical', where writers see life as problematic and express this in a philosophical and semi-philosophical way; 'Baroque', a sensuous ornate style, aiming at a startling form of expression.[2] What is confusing here is the use for one of the styles of a term now accepted as a designation for the period. Frank Warnke has suggested the following variation:

The term 'baroque' is relatively new to literary history, and there is notoriously little agreement on its proper denotation. I think it can most profitably be used as a generic designation for the style of the whole period which falls between the Renaissance and the neoclassical era; most modern readers agree in finding a period quality in the literature of the late sixteenth century and the first two-thirds of the seventeenth, and 'baroque' suggests this quality better than 'seventeenth century' or 'late Renaissance'. As the designation of a period, 'baroque' refers not to a precisely definable style but to a cluster of related styles. One of them is the Metaphysical; another is that curious phenomenon, as much social as artistic, known as préciosité. One is left with that group of poets most often called simply 'baroque'—Giles Fletcher, Marino, Góngora, D'Aubigné, Gryphius, Vondel—practitioners of a style marked by sensuous imagery, exclamatory syntax, and an attempt to achieve the stupefying and marvelous, a style which is more a hyperextension of Renaissance techniques than a revolt against these techniques. Such poets adhere to a precisely definable style which is neither Metaphysical nor Précieux, and their style deserves a name. One might use the term 'High Baroque'.[3]

Though this division seems neat it is really more confusing than helpful. 'Précieux' may certainly stand as a baroque style, provided it is understood in a sufficiently wide sense. 'Metaphysical', according to the now classical definition by James Smith, has come to be too restricted a term to be readily applied to literatures other than English.[4] With it is associated the conceit; conceits abound in Góngora, but *Polifemo* would not qualify as a metaphysical poem in James Smith's sense. For him metaphysical poetry is poetry dealing with metaphysical propositions and employing the 'metaphysical conceit', which is distinguished from the 'baroque conceit': the former holds the poem together, controlling and unifying its context by solving the particular metaphysical problem, whereas the latter, once stated, falls apart, and serves no other purpose than that of mere ornamentation.[5] Neither type of conceit covers those of *Polifemo*. The unsatisfactory nature of Warnke's definition of the three baroque styles is that Góngora is 'précieux' (in the broad sense), and also

(9)

'metaphysical' since he uses conceits organically, as well as being 'High Baroque' *par excellence.*

Leaving on one side the untransferable 'Gongorism', Spanish literature is fortunate in having only two basic terms by which to refer to baroque literature, *culteranismo* and *conceptismo*; each has variants and synonyms, *agudeza* and *ingenio* being the most important contemporary terms associated with the latter.[6] The belief, once universally held, that these are two antithetical styles, *culteranismo* being a poetic style that indulged in a florid play with words, while *conceptismo* was a prose style that ingeniously played with ideas, is no longer tenable. There is no necessary opposition between the two styles, but there is a clear differentiation.

Culteranismo is an intended ennoblement of the language of poetry by approximating Spanish to Latin in vocabulary and syntax far beyond the limits permissible in normal literary style, and by prodigally using rhetorical figures, especially hyperbole. On solemn occasions, such as commemorative orations and sermons, the language of prose was given this kind of ornamentation. In Góngora's hands this erudite and classicizing style has an achieved aesthetic purpose not covered by *préciosité*, but in lesser poets it can decline towards or fade into the pedantic affectation that this term denotes. This is, in fact, how it struck many of Góngora's contemporaries, especially the literary theorists and rhetoricians. The term *culterano* was almost certainly coined on the analogy of *luterano* (Lutheran), and its exponents were frequently referred to as a 'sect'. In so far as this style had a social basis it was not the product of a particular coterie but rather a cultural class distinction, the consciousness on the part of the sophisticated of constituting an élite distinct from the general literate public.

Góngora's *culteranismo* was not a bolt-from-the-blue in 1613 but the cultivation of a steadily developing aesthetic, after the introduction of Petrarchism into Castile, that idealized poetry as an inspired art appealing only to a select minority. Beginning with Fernando de Herrera's Commentary (1580) on the poems of Garcilaso,[7] this development constitutes a Platonic poetic stressing the 'divine madness' of the poetic imagination against the Aristotelian discipline of rules.[8] A landmark is the *Cisne de Apolo* by Luis Alfonso de Carballo (1602).[9] He harmonizes the Aristotelian concept of imitation with the Platonic 'madness': one cannot excel as a poet or artist without *ingenio*, which is intellect suffused by a creative and subtle imagination (*sutil imaginativa*). This poetic is given its fullest expression during Góngora's lifetime in the *Libro de la erudición poética* (1611) by his younger contemporary Luis Carrillo y Sotomayor (1583–1610), a highly gifted poet whose promise was cut short by an early death. This advocacy of an erudite poetry is fittingly given a Latin title, *Liber unus de Eruditione Poetica, seu tela Musarum, in exules indoctos a sui patrocinio numinis*;[10] it is a defence of the Muses against the unlearned, who are banished from their protection. This short treatise is not a theory of poetry but the manifesto of what came to be called the *secta de los culteranos*. Clarity, if it means making oneself intelligible to the half-educated, is a vice, not a virtue. The more difficult and hermetic a poem, the more pleasure it will give to a mind learned and sharp enough to unravel its meaning. For poetry delights not only the ear but the mind, and the mind must be given the stimulus of difficulty if it is to be left satisfied. This is the reply that Góngora would shortly afterwards give to those who accused him of being unintelligible. The defence of learned poetry was part of the aesthetic of the period in all countries: nobody, it was held, could be a great poet if he were not an erudite man.

A learned poetry meant for Carrillo a learned language as well as a learned matter. The Romans enriched their language by borrowing Greek words and expressions, why should not the Spanish of poetry be ennobled above everyday speech by drawing on both classical languages? But poetry should also be recondite because of the thought it expresses. Here *culteranismo* and *conceptismo* join hands. Conceptual subtlety as well as poetic erudition are the hall-mark of the highest art: both aim at the recondite because of the special intellectual pleasure provided by its elucidation. Carrillo anticipates Gracián's terminology: *agudeza* is synonymous with the intellectual difficulty he advocates, and the cultured and learned mind that grasps it is an *agudo entendimiento*. *Culteranismo* and *conceptismo* are therefore two closely allied ways of obtaining a single aesthetic-intellectual end.[11]

Agudo, the adjective on which the noun *agudeza* is formed, means 'sharp', 'keen'. The Italians used *acuto* and *acutezza* in the same literary context. In each language the noun denoted both the acuteness of the mind and an acute thought or pointed expression. The latter was also a *concepto*; this particular sense probably derived from Italian, where *concetto* was given this meaning much earlier; the English equivalent was and is 'conceit'. *Conceptismo* came into currency later as a synonym for *agudeza*, and has replaced it as the general term for this literary movement. In some ways this is unfortunate, since *conceptismo* implies a series of *conceptos*. *Agudeza* has no such implication: it is a quality of mind and a way of thinking which may, but need not, utilize the particular type of metaphor called a conceit. The best English equilavent for *agudeza* is the Elizabethan Wit (which will here be used throughout, capitalized, in this sense). Conceits are not essential manifestations of Wit, though they generally are its most striking form of expression.

Agudeza and Wit are not of course confined to the seventeenth century. Gracián, the great anthologist of Wit, finds examples in Latin literature (especially Martial), among the Fathers of the Church (especially St Augustine), in the Spanish courtly-love poetry of the fifteenth century and throughout the sixteenth. It is a recurring mode of thought and expression, which returned with special persistence in the seventeenth century. What was novel in the baroque age were particular forms of Wit and the theories of literature based upon it. These were themselves an attempt to explain and rationalize an already widespread fashion. Whereas sixteenth-century treatises on literary style had stressed the doctrine of imitation, the differentiation of the three styles and the principle of decorum, the seventeenth-century theorists all stress *acutezza* and the *concetto*. These treatises begin with the notes taken before 1640 by a student attending the course of lectures on *De arguto et acuto* at the University of Cracow by the Jesuit poet and professor of rhetoric, Matthew Casimir Sarbiewski (1595–1640),[12] who stated that while in Italy he had often discussed this subject with other Jesuit professors of rhetoric. The published treatises, in order of publication are: Matteo Peregrini, *Delle acutezze* (1639); Baltasar Gracián, *Arte de Ingenio* (1642); Sforza Pallavicino, *Trattato dello stile e del dialogo* (1646); Gracián, *Agudeza y arte de ingenio* (1648, a revised and expanded version of the *Arte* of 1642); Peregrini, *I fonti dell' ingegno* (1650); Emanuele

Tesauro, *Il cannocchiale aristotelico* (1654); Francisco Leitão Ferreira, *Nova arte de conceitos* (Lisbon 1718 and 1721).

It is no more easy to define Wit with any precision than it has proved easy to define the conceit. In general Wit is the intellectual agility that can see similarities in apparently dissimilar things, detecting 'correspondences' that are not self-evident, as well as the inventiveness that can express those 'correspondences' imaginatively. Addison's distinction between 'true Wit' (the association of ideas) and 'false Wit' (the association of words) has no validity for seventeenth-century practice or theory. The distinction, as always, is between good and bad, in relation to the particular context of the Wit in question. Wit and conceit are impossible to define exactly since their definition depends on differences of degree. There is no point on the scale at which it can be said that logical apprehension stops and Wit begins, or at which normal metaphors, or traditionally acceptable catachreses and oxymora, become conceits. One swallow does not make a summer, and a few examples of Latinization, strained comparisons or paradoxical expressions do not constitute a baroque style. Only where they pervade a work will they point to the seventeenth century, but this pervasion does not indicate any revolutionary change of taste or theory. There is an unbroken continuity from Petrarchism and Classical Humanism, and the taste for far-fetched metaphors and the treatises on Wit derive from Aristotle's definition of metaphor in the *Poetics* as 'an intuitive perception of the similarity in dissimilars', and from his *Rhetoric*, where metaphor is called 'a kind of enigma', and where 'clever enigmas' are said to 'furnish good metaphors'.

Góngora is both a *culterano* and a *conceptista*, in accordance with the aesthetic propounded by Carrillo. In him the elements of both styles are fused into an absolute artistic unity. In other poets the two styles are separable in practice. Quevedo, who with Calderón is the most profound exponent of a Wit in Spanish literature that can be called metaphysical in the narrow sense, was the most savage critic of the erudite and Latinizing features of Góngora's verse, which he ridiculed as pedantic affectation; he was, in other words, objecting to a *culteranismo* that he did not himself practise. Like Quevedo, Calderón and Gracián, nearly all the more important writers of the post-Góngora era are to varying degrees exponents of Wit. This fact, together with the standpoint of the theorists, indicates that Wit is the basic baroque style; *culteranismo* may or may not be an added ornamentation and refinement.[13] These rough-and-ready definitions have served to indicate the primacy and virtual universality of Wit; the characteristics of *culteranismo* and *conceptismo* will later emerge with greater precision from the analysis of *Polifemo*.

3. *Góngora's Life and Fame*

Don Luis de Góngora y Argote was born in Cordova on 11 July 1561 of noble family, the son of Don Francisco de Argote and Doña Leonor de Góngora. His preference for his mother's surname, while not exceptional in itself, would seem to accord with his sense of euphony and his predilection for proparoxytones; but it probably also proclaimed his indebtedness to his maternal uncle, Don Francisco de Góngora, who took charge of the boy's education. A prebendary of the Cathedral of Cordova, of lower status than a canon, Don Francisco ceded to Luis certain ecclesiastical benefices with revenues which he had in his possession, thus ensuring him a modest economic security, and sent him to the university of Salamanca, where he spent four years (1576–80) without taking a degree, having spent much of his time in literary pursuits and gambling. His earliest surviving poems can be dated 1580. On his return to Cordova his uncle resigned his prebend in Luis's favour, and the latter in order to qualify for it took minor orders up to deacon, with no intention of being ordained priest. The prebend entailed attendance in the cathedral choir at services and the recitation of the Office.

In 1587 a new bishop instituted an enquiry into the way the canons and prebendaries carried out their duties. Góngora was accused of being frequently absent from the cathedral services and, when present, of carrying on conversation instead of taking part in the prayers; of attending bullfights (which were forbidden to the clergy), associating with actors and writing frivolous and profane poems. He did not take the charges seriously and answered impenitently: he could not talk during the services even if he had wanted to, for on one side his neighbour was deaf and on the other side he never stopped singing; he appealed to his youth, asking not to be censured for living as a young man rather than an old one; he disowned the authorship of most of the poems attributed to him, but did admit to having written light verse, claiming his scanty knowledge of theology as his excuse, since he preferred to be condemned for frivolity rather than heresy. The bishop imposed a moderate fine as punishment and ordered him not to attend bullfights and to lead a more decorous life.

Shortly afterwards, Góngora began a series of journeys on business matters entrusted to him by the Chapter. In 1602 he was in Valladolid, where the Court was temporarily in residence; seven years later he was in Madrid. These visits introduced him to the highest literary circles and to the aristocratic milieu where his social tastes lay. He made friends at court: the Count of Villamediana, the Count of Lemos and the all-powerful Duke of Lerma. In 1611 he named a nephew as coadjutor of his prebend, which freed him from attendance at choir, but he continued to reside in Cordova, devoting himself to poetry. In May 1613 he gave the MSS of the newly completed *Polifemo* and the first part of the *Soledades* to a friend, Don Pedro de Cárdenas, to be taken to Madrid for circulation in literary circles.[14] In 1617 he fulfilled what must have been his ambition, to settle in Madrid. This was made possible by an appointment as royal chaplain, a post given him by Lerma; for this it was necessary to be ordained priest. He enjoyed the patronage of Lerma and of Don Rodrigo Calderón, Lerma's favourite, until both men fell from power in 1621 with the beginning of the new reign. Góngora sought the patronage of the new minister, the Count-Duke of Olivares, but this did not prevent him from being beset by economic difficulties. In 1627 he returned to Cordova, where he died on 23 May 1627.[15]

The impact that Góngora's fully-developed *culteranismo* made on the literary world in 1613 was mostly unfavourable. The new poems were stigmatized as incomprehensible, being in vocabulary and syntax more Latin than Spanish. This affectation of language was matched by the violence of the catachreses and the unending series of metaphors.[16]

It was a style that asked to be parodied and Quevedo, implacably hostile to Góngora, did not hold back. Two short skits of his are very funny: *La culta latiniparla* [The learned Latin-speaking Lady] and *Aguja de navegar culto, con la receta de hacer*

'*Soledades*' *en un día* [The Compass for Navigating Learnedly, with the Recipe for concocting *Solitudes* in one day]. The latter contains this poem, addressed to a woman's mouth:

Ejemplo hermafrodito : romance latín

> Yace cláusula de perlas,
>   si no rima de clavel,
>   dynasta de la belleza,
>   que ya cataclismo fue;
> un tugurio de pyropos,
>   ojeriza de Zalé,
>   poca porción que secuestra
>   corrusca favila al bien;
> pórtico donde rubrica
>   al múrice Tyrio el pez,
>   tutear padrón del alma,
>   aura genitiva en él.

Hermaphrodite specimen : vernacular Latin

> It lies there, a sentence of pearls, if not a rhyme of carnations, the Dynast of Beauty, which has already proved a cataclysm [to many]; a hut of carbuncles [or of flirtatious compliments], the envy of the [Moorish] Zalé; a small portion [of the woman] that sequesters the coruscating spark of happiness; an entrance porch that makes the Tyrian murex turn red with shame at the infamy to its soul, [when it sees] treated with such familiarity what in it is the breath of procreation [the colour purple].

There is extant an anonymous poem, *La Tormiada*, where the parody of *Polifemo* is so cleverly done that the reader is left with the uneasy feeling that his leg has been pulled and that the imitation is in fact seriously meant.[17]

Among the criticisms addressed directly to Góngora there is an anonymous letter from a man claiming to be a friend and expressing disapproval of the two new poems;[18] this is of interest only because a copy of Góngora's reply has survived. Though rather rude, it contains the only defence he offered for his art. In line with the 'Platonic' tradition of poetic theory, he claims that obscurity in poetry can serve a useful purpose. The struggle to construe Ovid's *Metamorphoses* sharpens and trains the minds of students: 'You will find the same thing in my *Solitudes* if you have the capacity to go beneath the surface in order to discover the mysteriousness they contain.'[19] He is writing for the learned, not the vulgar, and he is proud that his efforts have succeeded in raising the vernacular to the higher level and perfection of Latin. 'Moreover, it has been a matter of honour to me to make myself obscure to the ignorant, for that is what distinguishes the learned: to speak in a style that seems Greek to the ignorant, for precious stones should not be cast before swine.' He refuses to accept the criticism that his poetry is neither 'useful' nor 'pleasurable', but we should note that the pleasure he claims to provide is, like the 'usefulness', primarily intellectual:

> if the mind is given pleasure by being presented with statements that convince it and that are proportionate to its satisfaction, once it discovers what lies beneath those tropes the mind must necessarily be convinced and thereby satisfied. Moreover, since the final end of the intellect is to seize hold of truths (on which account nothing can [ultimately] satisfy it except the First Truth, in accordance with that saying of St Augustine: 'Our heart is restless till it rest in thee'), therefore, as the obscurity of the work compels the mind to ponder, its pleasure will be greater the more it discovers beneath the shadows of obscurity similarities with its own thought.

This last phrase has been found puzzling.[20] 'Similarities' is used to render 'asimilaciones'. 'Asimilar' could not in 1613 mean 'absorb and incorporate' (i.e. sensuous images into abstract thinking). Góngora must mean that the pondering (or speculation) of the mind can lead it to discover connexions between the poem's obscure images and its own ideas, thereby enabling it to accept the poem's statements as true; in other words, that the poem, precisely because of its obscurity, is food for thought in a satisfying way. This snobbishly intellectual view of poetry is not likely to predispose the would-be reader of *Polifemo* in its favour; but judgement should be suspended until one sees what kind of poetry is actually being defended in these terms. What should be noted in advance is that Góngora's 'ennoblement' of the language of poetry was in his own mind something more than linguistic refinement or sensuous ornamentation.

It is clear that he was deeply hurt by the hostility he aroused in 1613 and by the lampoons that followed. This may well be why the Third and Fourth *Soledades* were never written: he was too proud to cast any more pearls before swine. Not that admirers and defenders were wanting;[21] these recognized his serious artistic aims, and his reputation steadily grew, especially with the younger generation. After his death he came into his own. His Complete Poems were published in 1633.[22] The earliest commentary on *Polifemo* and *Soledades*, by Pedro Díaz de Rivas, must have been written before his death, but it remained unpublished. Between 1629 and 1648 there appeared six volumes of commentaries on these and other poems. Góngora thus achieved the status of a classic. Scarcely any poet who began to write after 1627 was untouched by his influence. Calderón moulded several features of Gongorism into a dramatic style of his own. Góngora was Gracián's favourite Spanish poet; he is represented far more copiously than any other in the latter's treatise on Wit.

The whole of baroque art suffered an eclipse in the eighteenth and nineteenth centuries. Some of the French Parnassians and symbolists, especially Verlaine, were fascinated by what they learned of Góngora but did not make his close acquaintance. The Modernist Ruben Darío began to bring Góngora back into favour among Spanish poets, a process that was accelerated when García Lorca raised his standard. The work of several scholars, with Dámaso Alonso to the fore, completed a revaluation that has remained unquestioned over a half century. Dámaso Alonso has in fact called Góngora the greatest European lyrical poet of the seventeenth century. Alonso's authority as a scholar and as a literary critic is beyond dispute; this statement must therefore command respect. It was not lightly made and could be weightily supported.

The past and present fame of Góngora contrasts ironically with that of his contemporary, Giambattista Marino (1569–1625), 'the Góngora of Italy' as Góngora is 'the Marino of Spain'. The Italian had a spectacularly successful career as a poet, nearly all of which he spent in courts, under the patronage of Cardinal Aldobrandini in Rome and Ravenna, of the Duke of Savoy in Turin, of the Queen-Regent in Paris and finally of the King of France. Everywhere he was honoured, esteemed and rewarded. His major work, *L'Adone*, was published in Paris in 1623; it had been long awaited and its appearance was an international sensation. His return to Italy was a triumphal march, he was fêted and acclaimed as the greatest living Italian poet, and on his death he was given a sumptuous funeral in his native Naples. Góngora might well have longed for such acclaim; had he received it he would surely have written more, or at least completed his major work. But perhaps his poetry, with its nostalgic sense of natural values in an externally beautiful world, and with the gravity given it by awareness of the transience of happiness, was made richer by the absence of court adulation and public lionization. However that may be, it is he, and no longer Marino, who can be called the greatest European poet of their century, for Marino's return to favour has been relative only.

4. *Wit and the Conceit*

The similarity between Marino and Góngora is superficially striking. The former is equally *culterano* in his lavishly expansive way; he too is prodigal with *acutezze*; and there are numerous points of contact in the balanced structure of their lines and stanzas and in the rhythms and euphony that both aimed at. Marino was of course as much read in Spain as he was elsewhere, and Góngora's commentators noted the occasional influence or borrowing. The similarity, however, comes from the Petrarchan tradition in its formal aspects, especially as developed in the sixteenth century. Both poets, as Dámaso Alonso has demonstrated from their manipulation of the *ottava rima*, represent the parallel culmination of this long tradition in their respective countries.[23] None-the-less, the differences between them are very great. Góngora is as compact as Marino is inordinately prolix; even more important, his Wit controls and unifies his themes, while Marino's is merely ornamental.

There is a further difference. Eugenio Donato has called Marino a revolutionary in one respect. Sixteenth-century poetics had been concerned with the difficult equilibrium between pleasure and morality, artifice and truth; with Marino these balances go by the board.

Marino's work can be briefly described as the highly metaphorical expression of highly sensual material—each of these terms being carried to such an extreme as to leave no doubt about its being treated as an end in itself.

The traditional standpoint had been that

If on the one hand the metaphor was pleasing, it served a moral purpose in teaching. If on the other hand it presented an artifice, that artifice was only a means of reaching a higher conceptual truth. But when the 'moderate-Baroque' critics of the next century had to face the poetry of Marino, it became apparent to them that the quality of artifice was not only pre-eminent but essential, and they were reduced to accepting metaphors as mere ornaments, not necessarily related to the poetical material . . . without danger of over-generalizing, one can say that the 'moderate-Baroque' critics came to accept a poetic in which the metaphor played a strictly orna-mental role, with the sole purpose of pleasing its audience.[24]

This is a modern way of expressing the problem which Marino's poetry posed for Italian critics and theorists. It certainly expresses the modern standpoint by which Góngora was revalued in the 1920s. There are indications that his opponents, in 1613 and subsequent years, were in fact troubled by this problem and not only by his Latinized language. Although modern critics have stressed—perhaps overstressed—Góngora's artifice, it cannot now be maintained that this has little contact with reality and human values, or that the *Soledades* and *Polifemo* do not exemplify a 'philosophical' view of life in the broadest sense. Certainly Gracián felt no need to justify any break with tradition in Góngora as Donato claims that Tesauro succeeded in doing with Marino.[25]

The point at issue is basically the distinction between the organic or functional conceit and the decorative conceit. An attempt at an aesthetic justification of *Marinismo* must entail dis-regard of the fact that such a distinction exists, but the distinction itself is basic for any discussion of the nature and function of Wit in the *Soledades* and *Polifemo*.

Another basic principle, which may conveniently be discussed first, is that Wit is independent of metaphor (i.e. of conceits). *Concepto* for Gracián means both the concept (idea or mental image) and its formulation in words, which need not be meta-phorical. His well-known definition of *concepto* is: 'An act of the understanding, that expresses the correspondence that exists between objects.' By 'objects' he understands not only material objects but also any object of thought: abstraction, attribute, relation (including coincidence, contradiction), etc. The verbal formulation of the concept is the 'objective' (and subtle) expression of the Wit. The latter is *artificiosa*, in the sense of not being the product of the intellect's natural functioning but an 'artistic' act of the *ingenio*—the intellect functioning imaginatively and aesthetically. An 'artificial' correspondence, says Gracián, is the determining feature of any kind of Wit: 'it embraces all the artifice of the mind, for although it may work through contrast and dissonance, that in itself is an artificial connecting of objects'.[26]

If we bear in mind that no definition in this sphere can ever be precise, it being impossible to say when intellectual apprehension ceases to be normal or logical and becomes artifice; if we also bear in mind, in consequence, that this definition is broad in all its terms, we are in a position to examine one of Gracián's simple examples and to find Wit where we suspected none. In one of Góngora's early poems, the ballad 'Entre los sueltos caballos' (1585), the vanquished Moor tells his captor how he had fallen in love in his boyhood with a girl who

Junto a mi casa vivía
porque yo cerca muriese.[27]
[She lived next door to my house
so that I might die close to her.]

Gracián finds 'many *conceptos*' in those two lines. First the significant reason behind the apparent coincidence of their living nextdoor to each other; secondly the parallelism of physical proximity (*junto*) and emotional union (*cerca*); thirdly the antithesis of her living so that he might die, this being, fourthly, an 'exaggeration', which for Gracián enhances the Wit, and fifthly a 'transmutation' from alive to dead. Disregarding the last two 'refinements', we can see how each of the three concepts establishes a 'correspondence'—a providential relationship between events, between two types of proximity in space and in the spirit, and between living and dying. These lines add no depth to the experience of falling or being in love, but they are very neat, all the more so for their remarkable simplicity. This neatness is aesthetically pleasurable; it is due entirely to the concise play of correspondences. These are themselves in harmony with the wider correspondences of the poem: the contrast between the tears of the absent lover and the valiant blows of the warrior; between the captivity of a lover and that of a prisoner of war; and between the soldier's gaining freedom in order to resume captivity. There is no profundity here, but the poem would not be so pleasing without these correspondences. Gracián finds 'many concepts' in these two lines, but there is no conceit. Even where, in his illustrations, tropes exist that can be called conceits, Gracián frequently takes them for granted in favour of the over-all Wit or some other aspect of it. For instance, he quotes these lines from *Polifemo*:

> al que con paso lento
> los bueyes a su albergue reducía,
> pisando la dudosa luz del día. (70-3).
> [of him, who plodding late
> To drive his cattle on their homeward way,
> Treads the uncertain light of dying day.]

'Uncertain' is not a literal translation of *dudoso*. Gracián comments in connexion with this word that 'every significant and appropriate adjective can serve the same purpose as a witty metaphor'.[28] He does not explain what he means, but we may note that *dudoso* signifies 'doubting' as well as 'doubtful'. This ambiguity can produce a double conceit; in the former sense it can be light doubting its own existence, and it can apply also to the wary herdsman; the adjective can thus act like a witty metaphor by uniting the man with the light on the same plane of insecurity. Gracián disregards (admittedly it is not in the context of this particular Discourse) the conceit of 'treading (or trampling) on the twilight'. This is surprising since 'the doubtful light' of twilight is not original: its source is Ovid's *Metamorphoses*, IV, 399-401 and XI, 595-6. It is also in Seneca, and Vilanova has recorded ten examples from Spanish, Portuguese and Italian Renaissance poets.[29] He found no other precedent, however, for the trope 'to tread (or trample) on the doubtful light of day' than in Góngora's own *Soledades* (I, 46):

> entre espinas crepúsculos pisando
> [Trod down the twilight in the thorny shade.]

This trope suggests treading warily, but also something more: as one treads down the embers of a dying bonfire, so each step one takes in the twilight, since with it the darkness increases, helps to extinguish the day. *Pisar* in this context may well be an example of what Gracián elsewhere calls 'a verb with depth':

> But the nerve centre of style lies in the intense profundity of the verb . . . The verb should be pregnant, not inflated; let it signify, not echo; verbs with depth of water where [the reader's] attention can put to sea, where his comprehension has something to grip and to feed on.'[30]

Another example where Gracián, quoting from *Polifemo*, finds the centre of the Wit outside the conceit is this:

> En carro que estival trillo parece,
> a sus campañas Ceres no perdona,
> de cuyas siempre fértiles espigas
> las provincias de Europa son hormigas. (141-4)
> [Ceres, her car a threshing-mill, decrees
> No respite to the produce of her soil,
> While from her fertile granary, like ants,
> The lands of Europe satisfy their wants.]

(Literally: 'Of whose ever fertile ears of wheat the provinces of Europe are the ants'.) Gracián does not call attention to the conceit 'provinces—ants' as a correspondence; he quotes this stanza in the Discourse on 'Wit through exaggeration', and gives it as an illustration of 'diminishing', or so to speak inverted, hyperbole. The stanza has exalted Sicily as 'the cup of Bacchus', 'the orchard of Pomona', the threshing-floor for Ceres's chariot, but at the end the provinces of the Roman Empire drop to the level of ants.[31] What strikes us about this metaphor for Sicily as the Granary of Europe, is its appositeness—the image of the restless activity of a busy port, with ships constantly arriving to pick up their cargoes and immediately departing; but what struck the theorist of Wit was the accentuation by the context of the element of surprise in the witty 'diminution' inherent in the hyperbolical comparison.

We are therefore dealing with a literary dimension beyond the reach of the formalist critic, stylistician or linguist. The structure of Góngora's metaphors has been studied by Bodo Müller, who has classified them according to 'grammar'. The resulting categories are based on relationships similar to those distinguished by the classical rhetoricians (genus—species; animate—inanimate, etc.). Such analysis cannot discern the Wit because it cannot 'go beneath the surface in order to discover the mysteriousness' contained, for instance, in this stanza of the *Polifemo*:

> Ninfa, de Doris hija, la más bella,
> adora, que vio el reino de la espuma.
> Galatea es su nombre, y dulce en ella
> el terno Venus de sus Gracias suma.
> Son una y otra luminosa estrella
> lucientes ojos de su blanca pluma:
> si roca de cristal no es de Neptuno,
> pavón de Venus es, cisne de Juno. (97-104)

> [He loves a nymph, daughter of Doris, fair
> Above all seen in Ocean's kingdom yet;
> Her name is Galatea, and in her
> Of Venus' Graces all the charms are met.
> Bright stars, both one and other, are the pair
> Of shining eyes in snow-white plumage set:
> If not a rock of crystal in the sea,
> Then Juno's swan or Venus' peacock she.]

This stanza interests Müller because of the 'ontological transference'. Galatea is transferred to three different orders of being: (1) divinity (*adora*), (2) the animal kingdom (swan and peacock), (3) inanimate Nature (rock). Only the vegetable kingdom is missing; but for this, says Müller, Góngora would at one stroke have transferred Galatea to all the ontological levels possible in the poetry of his age. Has this in fact anything to do with poetry? In lines 101-2 Müller expounds, within the class of 'predicative metaphor', the second, or 'defining', type. In the first, or 'comparing' type, the comparing particle is given, so the difference between the two objects remains. In the definition the particle is omitted, so the barrier of differentiation is broken down; no longer 'like' but 'is': there is complete identity between her 'shining eyes' and 'bright stars,' so that any attribute of the latter can be understood of the former.[32]

This is not the intellectual satisfaction Góngora expected his readers to derive from the investigation of what lay beneath his tropes. Galatea's eyes are the eyes on a peacock's tail; but they are set on white down, therefore on a swan; therefore she is both a peacock and a swan. In fact, she is Venus's peacock and Juno's swan; but how can this be, since the peacock was Juno's bird and the swan Venus's? The swan with peacock's eyes on its plumage, is a similar 'confusion'. What does all this mean? This is the 'mystery' that Góngora thought his readers would be stirred to ponder. A formal analysis of metaphors that disregards the conceptual relationships behind them cannot provide the answer. To look for the meaning behind the violence, paradoxes and 'impossibilities' of the correspondences is to give, as Gracián did, priority of analysis to Wit. By disregarding what the seventeenth century put in the centre, Müller comes to a misleading conclusion. Góngora, he says, is entirely traditional in his 'metaphorical themes'. He bases himself on the classical and Petrarchan heritage, and is an innovator who looks backwards, filling the poetic spaces left unoccupied by the current rules of poetry and thus exhausting all the possibilities in the Aristotelian canon.[33] On the other hand, we must add, what is forward-looking in Góngora is precisely the Wit, which organizes the traditional material of poetic metaphors into ordered and progressively developing conceptual structures, such as are not to be found in any sixteenth-century poet. The conceits in this stanza will be analysed later.

Exemplifying a totally different stylistic approach Dámaso Alonso sees 'pure *conceptismo*' as a formal technique that elaborates and complicates the words that 'signify' the ideas and not the ideas that are 'signified'. He concludes that the *conceptos* in Spanish seventeenth-century Wit are not, or only rarely, original or profound thoughts, but conventional ideas that are given ingenuity by the way they are expressed; it is a development not of content but of form.[34] This, without further qualification, may give rise to a misconception. It is true that the theorists of Wit maintained that an author's originality depended on 'form', since content, as such, was never original;[35] but by content they understood the ideas expressed in 'plain statement', i.e. in non-figurative language. 'Walking warily in the twilight' is a commonplace idea; 'trampling on the doubtful light of day' is a metaphor that is neither the same statement nor the same idea: it is a new, original and much more significant idea. The manner in which something is said conditions or alters what is said; metaphorical language does not just describe reality, it can change it. 'Imagination, stretches the mind, then, because it "stretches" reality by the linguistic means of metaphor. Given this, metaphor cannot be thought of as simply a cloak for a pre-existing thought. A metaphor is a thought in its own right.'[36] Wit, according to the theorists, *discovers* a significant relationship between objects and ideas that has always existed but has not previously been known. The novelty lies in the 'correspondence' by means of which the plain statement is given an original and a significant form.

Since the Wit of *Polifemo* cannot be analysed piecemeal, it is better to illustrate from another poem, different in every respect except the use of correspondences, how Wit transforms straightforward ideas into different thinking, enriching the thought without altering its basic meaning. Donne's 'Hymn to God, my God, in my sickness' will serve the additional purpose of illustrating the nature and range of the correspondences that, for Gracián, define Wit; it will also remind us that he is not writing of something that applies only to Spanish poetry.

> Since I am coming to that holy room,
>   Where, with thy choir of saints for evermore,
> I shall be made thy music; as I come
>   I tune the instrument here at the door,
>   And what I must do then, think now before.
>
> Whilst my physicians by their love are grown
>   Cosmographers, and I their map, who lie
> Flat on this bed, that by them may be shown
>   That this is my South-West discovery
>   *Per fretum febris*, by these straits to die,
>
> I joy, that in these straits, I see my West;
>   For, though their currents yield return to none,
> What shall my West hurt me ? As West and East
>   In all flat maps (and I am one) are one,
>   So death doth touch the Resurrection.
>
> Is the Pacific Sea my house ? Or are
>   The Eastern riches ? Is Jerusalem ?
> Anyan, and Magellan, and Gibraltar,
>   All straits, and none but straits, are ways to them,
>   Whether where Japhet dwelt, or Cham, or Sem.
>
> We think that Paradise and Calvary,
>   Christ's Cross, and Adam's tree, stood in one place;

Look Lord, and find both Adams met in me;
 As the first Adam's sweat surrounds my face,
 May the last Adam's blood my soul embrace.

So, in his purple wrapped receive me Lord,
 By these his thorns give me his other crown;
And as to others' souls I preached thy word,
 Be this my text, my sermon to mine own,
 Therefore that he may raise the Lord throws down.

'To tune an instrument' adds no philosophical or theological depth to the idea of preparation for death, but it is not the same idea: after death there will be an orchestral part to be played, before death one must get ready to play it. This is a difference of thought, not just of verbal expression. The correlation of music and heaven is as old as the concept of heaven itself, but does it not strike us here with a new force? The image of an orchestra tuning up before the appearance of the conductor, if we call it now to our minds, is no longer what it used to be.

Doctors diagnose an illness and judge whether the patient will die. To say that they are cosmographers (because they chart the patient's course) and he their map (on which they plot his course) is to think that idea in a different way. It is obvious that this applies to the whole poem: all of it is conceptual, not verbal, elaboration. The act of navigation having become a voyage of discovery, which direction shall it take? West is the direction of decline; south is the direction of the tropics (the heat of his fever: *fretum febris*), so his course is charted south-west. The south-westerly voyages of discovery had been the search for the sea-route to the Pacific—the straits of Magellan. But 'straits' (*freta*) are also tribulation, and to pass through them westwards into the suffering of death is to reach the East (the source of new life) since the West is the East on all maps that are laid out flat. Thus he is voyaging to Paradise.

Where is Paradise? In whatever part of the world it might have been, one must sail through the straits of suffering. If it is in Jerusalem (i.e. Mesopotamia), one must sail through the Straits of Gibraltar; if in the Pacific, then through the Bering Straits; if in India, then through the Straits of Magellan. According to the old legend Eden, the earthly Paradise, had been on the site of Calvary;

thus Christ's cross was raised over Adam's grave, where the Tree of the Knowledge of Good and Evil had grown. This correspondence is a 'mystery' to be pondered (in Gracián's sense). The legend itself arose precisely because the need of a correspondence was felt, namely a geographical link between Original Sin and the Redemption, and therefore between the two Adams. This geographical link had a theological correspondence. Death is the result of Original Sin; as each individual man dies and passes into Resurrection he fulfils the destiny of the human race, its beginning and its end. Both Adams meet in the dying poet. The last two lines of this fifth stanza are deeply moving. Adam's sweat is the agony of death; the blood of Christ is his redemptive sacrifice. These two lines would have greatly impressed Gracián. They exemplify what he would have called a Wit of 'double proportion', namely Sweat : : First Adam = blood : : Second Adam, and sweat : : face = blood : : soul. The crown of salvation can be won only with the crown of thorns. Man can enter heaven only if wrapped in Christ's purple cloak of majesty, which is the cloak of his blood.

The poem is a splendid example of continuously expanding and co-ordinated Wit; every new image and conceit is functional in terms of the total meaning. *Polifemo*, if it is a successful example of poetic Wit (in its very different pastoral, sensuous and erotic sphere) must be set against this standard of organic unity. It must also exemplify a comparably significant succession of correspondences.

Donne's poem is constructed in a continuous series of correspondences. It is about illness and death, but it covers music, cosmography, maps, the joining of west to east, voyages of discovery, searching for entries to other continents, doctors and their diagnosis, straits and fever, the location of Paradise. It then covers the essentials of Christian doctrine in the juxtaposition of Eden and Calvary, Adam and Christ, Original Sin and the Redemption, the fulfilment of human history by dying into resurrection. The effect of these correspondences is to bring an individual man on his deathbed into relation with all human activity (making music, charting new seas, discovering new continents) and into contact with human history and destiny (Adam, Noah, Christ). The lonely act of dying is made all-embracing. There is no parallel in any sixteenth-century poem of comparable length; there is here a larger vision in new, exciting imagery. For this baroque age there was no isolated individual. The whole world was bound together, each part of it, every human thought, every activity had a correspondence with every other. There was no 'absurdity': significant meaning was to be found everywhere and in everything. It was from poetry exemplifying this kind of Wit that the theorists extracted what has come to be called the Poetic of Correspondence.

This has often been called the product of a necessarily Christian Society, in which the poet's personal experience is of less interest than the collective experience manifested in the views of the world held by him in common with his readers. In such a society

the poet's task is ultimately one of discovering *God's* meaning, and his metaphors are means to that end. [So that the poet] draws attention, not to his own powers, but to God's who wrote the 'book' he is interpreting. The relationships that the metaphor establishes are created in the first place by God; the poet merely discovers them. As Miss Tuve puts it, the object of a metaphor of this sort is to reproduce the *intelligible* world; that is, the world that our intellects impose upon Nature, in accordance with our beliefs and our whole way of life. Given that, in a Christian society, the Deity is the focus of this way of life, Donne might well have regarded his metaphor as an instance of God's cleverness rather than his own. As a poet, he has, as it were, *discovered* the potential 'transference' between lovers and compasses, not *devised* it.[37]

Donne's 'Hymn to God, my God, in my sickness' is of course a perfect example of a poet expressing himself through the collective experience of a Christian society, but the identification of the Poetic of Correspondence with Christianity in general, or with Christian theology in particular, can be very misleading. Góngora did write poems that express a collective Christian experience, but far the largest part of his verse, including *Soledades* and *Polifemo*, is not even implicitly Christian (which does not mean that it is thereby anti-Christian), and if it is 'religious' at all, it exemplifies a religion of Nature. Tesauro did associate his poetic with what might loosely be called theology, but there is nothing of this in Gracián. Naturally the human intellect had for the latter an analogical relationship to the Divine Mind, and theological concepts offered a rich field for human Wit to exercise itself on, but his theory of Wit does not need Christianity or any theology for its basis, any more than does Góngora's exemplification of his own *agudeʒa*. Both lived in a Christian society and accepted its world-view, but the roots of the poetry are in classical mythology and the roots of the theory are in classical rhetoric.

5. Polifemo *and Gracián's Theory of Wit*

The phrase 'the poetic of correspondence' was coined by Mazzeo to denote the seventeenth-century treatises on Wit. It has been given currency by the frequent references to his valuable studies, but it has not helped to clarify the definition of Wit. An apparent disagreement on the definition of 'correspondence' has been made an excuse for dismissing Gracián's *Agudeʒa* from consideration in a book on the conceit:

> It was commonplace in the Renaissance to speak of the world as 'a universal and public manuscript' (*Religio Medici* [1643], I, xvi) containing sermons in stones and books in the running brooks, accessible to anybody with Browne's erudition and the patience of a cryptologist. God himself could be imagined as the archetypal concettist who created a world which St. Augustine calls an exquisite poem (*De Civitate Dei*, xi, 18), a poem full of occult correspondences, enigmatically impenetrable to undistinguished minds but an immensely rich hieroglyph to connoisseurs of the recondite. If God made poets in his own image they were bound to be concettists who would hold up the mirror to nature and subsequently load their poems with conceits either copied directly from those in the universe around them or constructed analogously. This is Mazzeo's approach to seventeenth-century poetry: for him, Metaphysical poetry mirrors an analogical universe in which everything has an occult connection with everything else . . .
> The treatise which has attracted most attention recently, however, is not by an Italian but a Spaniard, Baltazar [sic] Gracián. *Agudeʒa y Arte de Ingenio* . . . contains a definition of the conceit which seems conducive to a 'poetic of correspondence' such as Mazzeo supposes to have existed. A conceit,

says Gracián, is 'an act of the understanding which expresses the correspondence which is found between objects'. According to May, however, Gracián's *correspondencia* is not a metaphysical notion at all but 'refers to the reality expressed by all conceits' and derives 'ultimately from the scholastic idea of real proportional relations'... If May is right, then Mazzeo is wrong, although one can sympathize with Mazzeo's desire to treat *correspondencia* as an occult term like Baudelaire's *correspondances* and therefore interpret *Agudeza y Arte de Ingenio* as furnishing the otherwise missing metaphysic of Metaphysical poetry.[38]

There are several misrepresentations and misconceptions here. Mazzeo was not looking for a 'metaphysic of Metaphysical poetry' but for 'the theoretical basis of the "metaphysical" style so widespread in the poetry of the seventeenth century'. Nor did he see Gracián as expressing any 'metaphysical notion' or postulating a series of occult relationships in the universe; Mazzeo explained his 'correspondencia que se halla entre los objetos' as 'the hidden resemblances between things', hidden only until the Wit of the poet reveals them. Mazzeo's definition of what he calls 'the poetic of correspondence' is this:

> When the conceit is said to have those properties which enable it to pierce the intellect or to arouse sensations of marvel and wonder, we do wrong to think, as some critics have, of the more excessive kinds of Baroque art. What is meant is that quality of vision which the discovery of correspondences can bring, the 'thrill' which the awareness of an analogy gives the intellect when it first becomes aware of the identity between things formerly believed unconnected. The universe is a vast net of correspondences which unites the whole multiplicity of being. The poet approaches and creates his reality by a series of more or less elaborate correspondences.

The view of the universe and of poetic creativity expressed in the last two sentences was derived by Mazzeo, not from Gracián but from the later Tesauro. The theory of metaphor developed by Tesauro,

> was kept alive through the occult tradition, and reached Baudelaire through the agency of Swedenborg. It is not an accident that the great analogical complexity of much modern

poetry should have been largely the work of Yeats and
Baudelaire, two poets who studied the occult sciences and
who revived the conception of the poet as one who approaches
reality through the discovery of the analogies latent in nature.[39]
However that may be, the occult sciences do not underpin 'the
poetic of correspondence'. They are quite absent from Gracián,
whose attempt to expound a *Mind's Art*, i.e. an aesthetic, should
not be disparaged by such a misconception.

'Mind' is an inadequate translation of *ingenio*; for this Art to be
understood we must first grasp the basic distinction, previously
referred to in connexion with the poetic of Carballo, between
entendimiento (understanding) and *ingenio*. The distinction may be
more easily grasped if we first glance at its precedents. Though
Gracián's doctrine must derive directly from the Rhetoric taught
in Jesuit schools, of which Sarbiewski's *De acuto et arguto* is an
example, the concept of *ingenio* would seem to have deeper roots
in the medieval Platonic tradition, and so in certain aspects of the
Renaissance Philosophy of Nature.[40]

The thought of Nicholas of Cusa (1401–64) was governed by
'the idea of unity as the harmonious synthesis of differences'.[41]
This theory of knowledge distinguishes three stages. The lowest
stage is that of the senses, which simply affirm. The next stage is
that of reason (*ratio*), which distinguishes. Reason is governed by
the principle of contradiction: because a thing is this, it cannot be
that, hence opposites are mutually exclusive. The highest stage of
knowledge is that of intellect (*intellectus*), which synthesizes and
harmonizes. This is an activity of the mind superior to reason.
The intellect denies the oppositions of reason; the latter affirms
that A cannot be its opposite, z, but intellect can deny the separate-
ness of A and z because it apprehends God as the being in whom
opposites coincide, as the *coincidentia oppositorum*. This apprehen-
sion cannot be stated logically, because that is the language of
reason; intellect uses language to *suggest* meaning rather than to
state it, and employs analogies and symbols. (Gracián will make
the distinction between the language of plain statement, which is
that of the understanding, and the language of Wit, which is that
of *ingenio*, and to analogies and symbols he will add conceits.)

Nicholas of Cusa's idea of God is developed in *De docta
ignorantia* (paradox being at the heart of the language of intellect

as of *ingenio*). Things and creatures are multiple and distinct; God transcends all distinctions and oppositions, reducing them into the unity of his own being. In things and creatures we can distinguish the opposition of large and small, but in God these opposites coincide. He cannot be greater than he is, hence he is the maximum, but he also cannot be less than he is, hence he is the minimum. He is therefore both the greatest and the smallest in a perfect *coincidentia oppositorum*, and this statement is on that account a metaphysical conceit.

A further paradox describes the created world: it is the 'contraction' of infinity and unity (*infinitas contracta* and *contracta unitas*). God himself is all being in essential simplicity and unity. 'In the *explicatio Dei* or creation of the world unity is "contracted" into plurality, infinity into finitude, simplicity into composition, eternity into succession, necessity into possibility.'[42] Such paradoxes cannot be grasped by reason, which operates through logic; they are accessible only to the *intellectus* (or *ingenio*).

The Coincidence of Opposites, derived from Nicholas of Cusa, became the centre of the philosophy of Giordano Bruno (1548–1600), the most famous of the Philosophers of Nature.[43] This line of thought, important in the context of the Renaissance, whereby differences are transcended and disparity can become equality, must have influenced poets to invent images in which dissimilars were united in similarity. The widespread use of such imagery, neither analysed nor accounted for in manuals of traditional rhetoric, fired Gracián to devise a new 'Art'.

The first version of *Agudeza y arte de ingenio* was published in Madrid in 1642. Its full title was *Art of the Mind, Treatise on Wit. In which are explained all the Modes and Differences of Conceits*. Gracián's friend and patron, Don Vincencio Juan de Lastanosa, when he published the former's *El discreto* (1646), complained in his preface that an Italian had translated the *Agudeza* and passed it off as his own. The alleged culprit was Matteo Peregrini (or Pellegrini), whose supposed plagiarism, *Delle acutezze*, had actually been published three years before Gracián's treatise. In 1650, in the preface to *Fonti dell' ingegno* (Sources of Wit), Peregrini reversed the accusation, referring to the translation of his earlier work into Spanish by somebody who then not only claimed it as his own but boasted that it had been translated into Italian by

Peregrini himself. Neither writer had read the other's book. The two works are similar in their terminology and have several examples in common (doubtless due to common sources in Jesuit rhetoricians, Gracián being himself a Jesuit), but they are otherwise very different. Peregrini, being suspicious of the possible corruption of good style, is as cautious as Gracián is enthusiastic and confident of his case.

Agudeza y arte de ingenio is the title of the second version of Gracián's work (1648). In full it runs: *Wit and the Art of the Mind, in which are explained all the Modes and Differences of Conceits, with Examples, both Sacred and Profane, taken from all that has been best expressed.* This definitive version is considerably longer than the first; the new material includes sections on style and on the application of erudition to literature, as well as numerous new examples of witty writing, notably the skilful translations of Martial by his friend Manuel de Salinas, Canon of Huesca. It is a difficult work in thought, language, style and organization. Definitions, classification and terminology are cast in a scholastic mould and are not readily comprehensible to the unprepared reader. The difficulties of style are Gracián's own; he is not an easy author to read in any of his works. The presentation is diffuse and tends to be repetitive; the organization lacks logical order. In the second version the new material is often inserted in the middle of an expository passage, which is taken up again later. No reader should therefore embark on its study without guidance.[44]

Reason and logic are excluded from the *Agudeza* by definition. The activity of *ingenio* is the supra-rational activity of the *intellectus* of Nicholas of Cusa, and its language is not that of logical statement. Literature has its 'science', which is Rhetoric with its categories for classifying the various tropes, and its rules for their formulation and use. Gracián excludes Rhetoric in the first sentence of his Preface and claims to be breaking new ground with a 'novel theory' (*teórica flamante*), for although some of the subtleties of the art of Wit, 'like orphan children who do not know their real mother', have been fathered on Rhetoric, they have thereby revealed only shadowy glimpses of their real nature.[45] *Conceptos* have hitherto been considered the children of mental effort rather than of artistry (*artificio*); they have been born untutored, cast at random into a world where imitation took the place of art. All art stands in need of a guiding direction, most of all the art that consists in the subtlety of the mind (*ingenio*), and this direction is what Gracián is setting out to provide. Every faculty has a mode or modes of operation and each has an object proper to itself. The mind's highest operation is Wit (*agudeza*), and the proper object of Wit is the *concepto*. The understanding, if it lacks Wit and *conceptos*, is like the sun without rays and light (Disc. i; 1, 47–50). The *concepto* is to the mind what material beauty is to sight and what musical harmony is to hearing. To perceive Wit is to have the perspicacity of an eagle, but to produce it is to be like an angel, for it (i.e. the intuitive grasping of relationships and correspondences) is the operation of the Cherubim, and raises men to a hierarchy beyond the human norm.[46] Therefore the power of the mind to produce Wit is the highest form of human creativity; this is *ingenio*, the mind functioning at its highest level and producing its noblest object (Disc. ii; 1, 50).

The terms are by now sufficiently clear. *Agudeza* is both Wit in general and the intellectual faculty that perceives and produces it; *concepto* is the act of conception whereby correspondences are intuited; it is also the idea so formed, and the verbal expression in which the imagination embodies it. In other words, *concepto* according to the context is 'conception', 'concept' (or 'percept') and 'conceit'. Gracián distinguishes Wit from philosophical speculation on the one hand and from literary composition on the other. The artistry[47] of dialectic consists in the way premises and conclusion are formulated and connected in order to construct a good argument. The artistry in rhetoric consists in the adornment of language and the composition of tropes. *Ingenio*, unlike understanding, is not satisfied by truth alone, but aspires to beauty. The beauty that appeals to each faculty of sense consists in the artistry that combines and interrelates their objects in harmonious proportion. Even taste, the 'vulgar' sense, receives special pleasure from the skilful (*artificioso*) combinations of piquant and smooth, sweet and bitter. Concept and conceit are formed by the union of two 'knowable terms' (i.e. known by experience), and their beauty consists in the kind of correlation that brings them together, one whose pleasing subtlety surprises and delights the mind (i.e. by being new to experience):

The artistry of Wit therefore consists in a pleasing concordance, in a harmonious correlation between two or three knowable terms, the correlation being expressed by an act of the mind ... So that we may thus define the *concepto* [concept and conceit]: it is an act of the mind that expresses the correspondence that exists between objects ... The actual expression of the consonance or skilful [*artificioso*] correlation is the objective subtlety [i.e. the conceit] ... This correspondence is generic to all concepts [or conceits] and embraces all the artistry of the *ingenio*, for although this may take the form of contrast and dissonance, this too is an artistic [*artificioso*] connexion of objects.[48]

Such is Gracián's general exposition of Wit. This is followed by a classification of its principal types and of the variety of modes within each type. The unique value of the *Agudeza* lies in the very large number of examples that illustrate each type and mode, and in the analysis of what comprises the Wit in each example. These range from complete poems with profound conceits down to mere ingenious witticisms or plays on words. We find it hard to see all these examples as equally beautiful, but Gracián does not differentiate or grade quality, although some of his examples earn higher praise than others. His intellectual beauty is analogous to the beauty a mathematician finds in the neatness and elegance of a proof, or the satisfaction logicians used to find in disputations conducted in skilful and concise syllogisms, despite the lack of any profound significance in the subject argued.

It must not be thought, however, that this is the whole of beauty for Gracián, or that the only pleasure he and his contemporaries expected the reader to find in *Polifemo* lay in the detection and elucidation of far-fetched correspondences. A man who saw art in the varied combinations of flavours in cooking, will not be insensitive to or expect his readers to overlook the beauty that appeals to the senses. This, however, is not the subject of his book, so he takes it for granted and proceeds to add to what is already known an extra aesthetic dimension not yet properly perceived or understood. That we may be reluctant nowadays to call beautiful anything that is purely intellectual should not affect his argument or the value of his work as an analysis of the aims and techniques of the writers of his age. For we can derive a certain intellectual satisfaction or pleasure (or understand how others might derive it) from the ingenuities and subtleties of their writings. None-the-less, the 'art of the mind' is not to be interpreted as a purely cerebral poetry, but as an added refinement to the pleasure afforded by the traditional 'adornment' of language. In order to avoid misconceptions at the outset it might be appropriate, before embarking on Gracián's classification of Wit, to indicate from some simple examples what kind of aesthetic appeal accompanies the Wit of *Polifemo*.

When Galatea is lying asleep by the stream, and Acis, after leaving his offering beside her, cools his face with the water, its splashing wakens her:

Vagas cortinas de volantes vanos
corrió Favonio lisonjeramente
a la de viento, cuando no sea cama
de frescas sombras, de menuda grama. (213-16)

(Literally: 'Caressingly the West Wind drew back the flimsy curtains of airy veils from around the bed—one of wind [hammock], if not a bed of short grass and refreshing shade.') To waken a sleeper by drawing back the curtains of her bed is the trope which is the starting point for the conceit. The line describing the curtains has a balanced rhythm in the chiasmus adjective-noun-noun-adjective, and in the triple alliteration of *v-s*. Balance, rhythm and alliteration give it a lovely sound, and this sensuous beauty first captures the ear. But the mind asks, what are these curtains? The image is one of gently fluttering, gauze-like fabric, and this is a sense-impression that adds body to the verbal beauty. But the curtains are not only drawn back by the wind, they are the wind, and so non-existent—transparent and invisible, their fluttering being seen only as the wind rustles the trees and ripples the grass. The bed itself is thus a 'wind-bed'—not indeed a hammock, but a shady patch of soft grass curtained by the breeze. The conceit is thus an intellectual investigation ('ponderation' is Gracián's term) of the congruity behind the apparently incongruous term for hammock—'a bed made of wind'. The creation of the folding veils and their dissolution into airy nothingness add greatly to the melodic beauty of the lines; they are what Wit contributes to the poetry.

Golden honey glinting as the sun strikes it is turned by Wit into:

troncos me ofrecen árboles mayores,

cuyos enjambres, o el abril los abra,
o los desate el mayo, ámbar distilan
y en ruecas de oro rayos del sol hilan. (397–400)

(Literally: 'The tallest trees offer me their trunks, in which my swarms of bees wakened by April or released by May, distil amber and spin sunbeams on golden distaffs.') The correspondences honey—linen thread, sunbeams—flax, honey comb—distaff, are so remote that only Wit can bring them together. The beautiful image of the golden honey glistening in the sun and drawing its shimmering texture from the latter's rays is sensuous poetry, but this beauty would not exist but for the 'art of the mind', which alone could conceive of the thin streams of honey pouring out of the cells of honey combs as thread being spun from a distaff. It is clear, therefore, that Gracián's *ingenio* is not pure reason, but reason pervaded by imagination, and thus creative of poetry, not of discourse.

Since the object of *ingenio* is beauty, not scientific truth, its *agudeza de artificio* is distinguished from the *agudeza de perspicacia* which characterizes philosophers and scientists—the clarity of mind that can perceive and analyse relations and differences that are logical and objectively true. 'Perspicacity' and 'artifice' thus divide the activity of the mind.[49] The first general division Gracián makes of the Wit of artifice is between 'simple' (*incomplejo*) and 'compound' (*compuesto*). 'Simple' Wit is a single conceit; though it can give rise to a number of secondary conceits through the exploration of its adjuncts,[50] it is based on a single concept. 'Compound' Wit is a construction based on many conceits, united by the artistic structure of the work or its theme; this he compares to a building constructed not with columns and architraves, but with motifs and concepts.[51] Here Gracián is suggesting the 'organic conceit', which in conjunction with others contributes to the over-all unity of the work of which they are functional parts. *Polifemo* will be an example of Compound Wit if among the multiplicity of simple conceits that give 'ornamentation' to the fable there are some that fall into groups forming continuous strands in the poem's structure.

Gracián's classification of Simple Wit is over-elaborate. For the purpose of analysing *Polifemo* it can be simplified into these general types, retaining his own terminology:

A 1. Correspondence and Proportion ⎫
A 2. Disproportion and Dissonance ⎭
B 1. Similarity ⎫
B 2. Dissimilarity ⎭
C 1. Parity ⎫
C 2. Disparity ⎭

Examples will be selected from *Polifemo* to illustrate each of these six types in turn.

A1. *Correspondence and Proportion.* Proportion, for Gracián, is the first and paramount type of correspondence. *Proportio* was used in Latin to translate the Greek *analogia*; Gracián's use of it must be sought in the scholastic doctrine of analogy. Aquinas deals with this in his discussion of the names of God,[52] but the development of the doctrine was due to the *De nominum analogia* of Cajetan (Thomas de Vio, 1468–1534).[53] The same predicates are affirmed of different subjects, or the same adjectives qualify different nouns, in three different ways: univocally ('men are human', 'women are human'), equivocally ('a right answer', 'a right turn'), and analogically. Three types of analogy are distinguished. The first, that of inequality, is not properly analogy. 'Men are animals' and 'dogs are animals': though there is a higher degree of perfection in human animality, the definition of the term covers both men and dogs; it is therefore used univocally, and to call this analogy is inexact. Secondly, there is analogy of attribution. 'A man is healthy' and 'milk is healthy'; in the first case health is possessed formally, in the second it is attributed because milk preserves or restores health. This is improper analogy, but admissible 'on sufferance'. True analogy is the third type, that of proportionality. Proportion signifies equality of ratios, as in mathematics (2 is to 4 as 12 is to 24; or 5 is to 15 as 20 is to 60). Outside mathematics it is the comparison of things that are in some respects different and in others the same; the comparison is therefore neither univocal nor equivocal. Non-mathematical proportions are either metaphorical or non-metaphorical. 'The lion is the king of beasts' means that the lion is to beasts as a king is to his subjects; this proportion is stated as a metaphor and this kind of correspondence provides the basic metaphors of poetry. Analogy of proportionality in the proper philosophical sense occurs where there is predication or comparison without the use of metaphor. 'God is wise' and 'a man is wise'; wisdom is to man as wisdom is to God: there is analogy of proportion without metaphor. Gracián had no need to explain all this; it was familiar already to any reader educated enough to understand *Agudeza*. We may now apply these definitions to *Polifemo*.

Every conceit is based on a metaphor, but in well-developed ones the metaphor is concealed or elliptically expressed. In stanza 35 of *Polifemo* Galatea, looking at Acis who is feigning sleep, is attracted by his hair and the down on his cheeks. These are 'the snake in the grass' which will administer love's poison to her. His untidy hair and beard are more attractive than would be the spruced appearance of a fashionable young man. So stanza 36:

> En la rústica greña yace oculto
> el áspid, del intonso prado ameno,
> antes que del peinado jardín culto
> en el lascivo, regalado seno   (281–4)

(Literally: 'The serpent lies hidden in the rustic unkempt locks of the pleasant unshorn meadow, rather than in the exquisitely pleasing bosom of the well-combed cultivated garden.') To say, as most commentators do, with the exception of Vilanova, that *intonso* and *peinado*, applied to *prado* and *jardín*, are used in the figurative senses found in Latin poetry, is to miss the Wit of Proportion in these two stanzas. The double analogy is: uncut hair is to a face as unmown grass is to a meadow, and combed hair is to a head as cultivation is to a garden. If the analogy had been explicitly stated—'his unkempt locks were an unmown meadow, (in the previous stanza his downy beard was 'flowers') 'and not the combed hair of a cultivated garden' (that the one is the opposite of the other is an added witty correspondence)—the metaphors would doubtless be far-fetched enough to count as conceits. But with the metaphors implied or only half-stated, and in the wider context of the colour of the setting sun, of the closed eyes and of love's potion, we have a complex example of what Gracián called the Wit of Proportion; its *artificio* is singularly satisfying and also sensuously beautiful.

Gracián describes this first type of Wit in these words:

> The subject to be pondered and reflected on [e.g. the erotic attraction of Acis's hair and beard] ... is a sort of centre from which the reflecting mind draws lines of thought and subtlety

to the entities that surround it, that is to say the adjuncts that crown it, such as its causes, its effects, its attributes, qualities, contingencies, circumstances of time, place, mode etc., and any corresponding term; the reflecting mind proceeds to compare them one by one with the subject, and with each other; and when it discovers some conformity or correlation, either in relation to the subject or among the adjuncts themselves, it expresses and stresses this correlation, and in this consists the subtlety . . . So that this first type of Wit consists in a certain harmony and pleasing correspondence that the terms have between themselves or with the subject . . . When this correspondence is hidden and needs to be worked out in order to be detected, it is the more subtle the greater the effort entailed . . . this mode of conceit is called proportional because it is concerned with the correspondence between the knowable terms.[54]

Metaphorical proportions are numerous in *Polifemo*. A simple example is the rock which closes Polyphemus's cavern; this 'muzzles its mouth':

> Allí una alta roca
> mordaza es a una gruta, de su boca. (31-2)

More complex and witty is the straw in which pears are stored until they ripen into a golden colour. This is a 'pale-faced guardian', jealously keeping her female ward from the sight of men until she is ripe for marriage and 'gilded' with a dowry:

> la pera, de quien fue cuna dorada
> la rubia paja, y—pálida tutora—
> la niega avara, y pródiga la dora. (78-80)

(Literally: 'the pear whose golden cradle was the blonde straw, which she, a pale guardian, hoards miserly while prodigally gilding it/her.') The implications of the conceit straw—tutor (Gracián's 'adjuncts') are that the girl was born into wealth; while she is being brought up in seclusion, this wealth is being hoarded; at the same time nature is enriching her with beauty by maturing her into womanhood. To the initial correspondence straw—guardian, we have the added progression storing > ripening > gilding, which produces at the end the chiastic contradiction between 'hoarding miserly' and 'prodigally endowing'. This last adjunct to the conceit is an example of the second type of Wit.

A2. *Disproportion and Dissonance.* This is the counterpart to the first type. Instead of a harmonious correspondence between the terms of the conceit, what is sought is opposition or disharmony. Beauty, says Gracián, lies in proportion, only rarely is it found in disproportion in actual fact, but to note and express it gives perfection to Wit. This dissonance, he says, is much practised by writers because there is no difficulty in conceiving it. The greater the incompatibility between the two terms the greater the Wit, and an especially pleasing harmony is produced by the mingling of proportion and disproportion in the same conceit.[55]

From the examples Gracián gives it is clear that dissonance covers simple contrast as well as open contradiction. He singles out Góngora as the master in this type of conceit: 'This *culto* poet was a swan in his harmonies, an eagle in his conceits, eminent in every kind of Wit; but the triumph of his great genius consisted in this Wit of counter-proportions: his works are interlaced with this subtlety'.[56] The examples given are taken from Góngora's lyrics, but *Polifemo* reveals how exact it is to speak of interlacing, so abundant are these disproportions.

Polyphemus climbs a rocky cliff from the top of which he sings his song. This rock is like a lighthouse or a watch-tower on the shore. This is not a simple simile but a proportion, as the context discloses, because the giant's single eye is so brilliant that it rivals the sun (lines 421–4); this, as he stands on the rock, is the light of the lighthouse. From the top of it he commands a wide view and as he sees Acis running away his roar presages his death (lines 481–8). There is proportionality, therefore, between Polyphemus on his rock and a lighthouse—watchtower. But the rock itself has no light and no means of sounding an alarm: it is therefore 'a blind light and a dumb watchtower' [linterna es ciega y atalaya muda] (344). The constant doubling of this type of conceit—with a noun + adjective structure, either repeated as here, or in chiasmus as in the previous and the following examples—emphasizes the disproportion.[57] This, in effect, constitutes a conceptual and stylistic convention that Góngora imposes on himself, and as such one may come to take it for granted when it appears.

Galatea lying asleep by the side of the stream rivals in the transparent whiteness of her skin the limpidity of the water: both are 'crystal', but one is 'murmuring' and the other 'silent'. Both, however, are equally refreshing to Acis, but it is his parched mouth that is refreshed by the one and his sight by the other:

> su boca dio, y sus ojos cuanto pudo,
> al sonoro cristal, al cristal mudo. (191–2)

(Literally: 'he gave his mouth—and, as far as he could, his eyes— to the sounding crystal, to the dumb crystal'.) In addition to the basic dissonance of the crystal that is both sonorous and dumb, the conceit depends upon the contrast (a disproportion) between mouth and eyes.

One day, when Polyphemus was on his rock, the sea was so calm that he could see side by side the reflections of his single eye in the middle of his forehead and of the sun in the middle of the sky:

> Miréme, y lucir vi un sol en mi frente,
> cuando en el cielo un ojo se veía:
> neutra el agua dudaba a cuál fe preste,
> o al cielo humano, o al cíclope celeste. (421–4)

(Literally: 'I looked at [my reflection] and saw a sun shining on my brow when an eye could be seen shining in the sky: the water, undecided, doubted to which it should give credence, whether to the human heaven or to the heavenly Cyclops'.) The proportion between sun and brow, eye and sky, contains within itself the disproportion (which Gracián would have found especially witty because of the extreme incompatibility) between human and celestial.

B1, 2. *Similitude and Dissimilitude.* These two types and their various modes are dealt with in Discourses ix–xii. Gracián says that not everyone would agree in distinguishing this type of conceit from the rhetorical figure (i.e. simile). His meaning becomes clear enough from the numerous examples he gives, though some of them might seem to stretch the distinction too fine. He defines similitude as Wit in which a subject is not compared with its own adjuncts, but with an unconnected term, such as an image which expresses the nature of the subject or represents the subject's adjuncts. Sarmiento explains this as follows:

> [Similes] are the ground, the matter for the formation of the conceit, [but] to constitute it there must be a second justifying reason for the simile, which is brought out (understanding

of course that the reason may be poetical or fanciful only),
or else that the simile is established between terms that at
first sight offer no ground, real or easily imagined, for such an
approximation.[58]

In lines 313–14 the grass on which Acis and Galatea will recline
is likened to a carpet dyed with the richest Tyrian colours:

Sobre una alfombra, que imitara en vano
el tirio sus matices
[Reclined upon a carpet rivalling
The Tyrian hues for splendour,]

But it is Nature that is being compared to the Tyrian craftsman:
she is thus the silk worm who spun the thread and the artist who
wove the carpet. This is the second justifying reason for the trope,
and what transforms it into a conceit:

(si bien era
de cuantas sedas ya hiló, gusano,
y, artífice, tejió la Primavera)
[though it still
Was made from threads which like a silkworm, Spring
Had spun, and woven with an artist's skill,]

An example of Gracián's dissimilitude would be the fourth
stanza of Polyphemus's song:

Pastor soy, mas tan rico de ganados,
que los valles impido más vacíos,
los cerros desparezco levantados
y los caudales seco de los ríos;
no los que, de sus ubres desatados,
o derivados de los ojos míos,
leche corren y lágrimas; que iguales
en número a mis bienes son mis males.   (385–92)
[A shepherd I, with flocks so well supplied
They hide the mountain tops, however high,
They fill the valley beds, however wide;
The largest river, when they drink, runs dry.
Not so the streams that from their udders glide,
Nor those that draw their waters from my eye—
Torrents of milk and tears, whose volume shows
My goods are matched in numbers by my woes.]

The flow of tears from Polyphemus's eyes (Góngora forgets, on this occasion, that he has only one) would be like the flow of water in the rivers, but for the fact that the tears never dry up. His prosperity, measured by the multitude of his flocks, dries up the rivers, but this prosperity, is by contrast, manifested in the unceasing flow of milk from the udders. The original comparison is thus extended into the further comparison of eyes to udders and tears to milk, which then leads into the dissonant equality (*iguales*) of the antonym *bienes—males* ('good'—'evil'). The dissimilitude of the total conceit is thus the contrast between the disharmony of unending human sorrow within the ceaselessly creative fertility of nature.

C1, 2. *Parity and Disparity*. What is denoted here is the equality of two things in importance, in their operations or effects, etc., or a corresponding inequality, rather than the resemblance that is the basis of similitude. Polyphemus's gaping cavern is like the earth 'yawning' (41–2), and the rock that closes it is like a 'muzzle' over its 'mouth' (32); his long unkempt beard flowing in disorder down his huge chest 'looks like' a waterfall, an 'impetuous torrent' (61). These are the resemblances that produce normal similes, and the significance of these tropes does not go beyond the resemblances. But when Góngora says that Cupid pierced Galatea's heart with an artist's paintbrush (not with a dart), he is indeed making a comparison that starts from similarity of size and shape, but the comparison does not depend upon this but upon the similar result each produced:

A pesar luego de las ramas, viendo
colorido el bosquejo que ya había
en su imaginación Cupido hecho
con el pincel que le clavó su pecho,   (269–72)

(Literally: 'Then seeing in colour, despite the branches, the sketch that Cupid had done in her imagination with the brush with which he pierced her heart'.) Before seeing Acis Galatea had imagined what he might look like; this 'brushwork' had been the piercing with the dart which had predisposed her to fall in love, as she did when she actually saw him. This is 'parity', not 'similitude'. Gracián of course insists, as he did with the latter type of conceit, that there must be some special element in the comparison, or some special reason for it, to make it Wit and not just trope. Discourses xiv–xvi cover this type.

Other examples of parity are the sun horse, Aethon, 'his breath smoke, his neighs fire' [Su aliento humo, sus relinchos fuego] (337) when by metonymy he stands for the sun itself. Or Galatea, when she 'became the scythe of her own lilies', [segur se hizo de sus azucenas] (220). Reclining on the ground her white form had been a bed of lilies; by jumping up she scythed them down. Since this makes her the destroyer of her own beauty the conceit can be considered as an example of disparity.

Such are the main types of conceits that are based on metaphors. This represents only a small part of *Agudeza y arte de ingenio*, which is a veritable tour-de-force with its sixty-three Discourses covering every conceivable type of Wit in arguments, enigmas, allusions, allegories, puns etc. Though the complete work is very relevant to seventeenth-century literature, only the above summary is relevant to *Polifemo*. It will be fitting to conclude this brief survey of the work by some quotations from the closing section:

> Two things make a style perfect, the verbal matter and the intellectual form,[59] for its perfection depends upon the proper harmony between these two powers. Some are content with the soul of Wit alone, disregarding splendour in its expression; rather do they take simplicity of diction, even in poetry, as the mark of excellence ... Words are what the leaves are on trees, the *conceptos* being the fruit. It was not paradox but ignorance that condemned all *conceptos*. Neither was it Aristarchus who criticized Wit[60], but a monster: the antipode of *ingenio*, whose mind must have been the desert of discourse. *Conceptos* are the life of style, the soul of speech, whose perfection is proportional to its subtlety. Elevation of style united to loftiness of *conceptos* makes a work perfect ... [But this union must contain] a grain of tact, for everything is seasoned by good judgement. What applies to rhetorical figures is applicable also to conceits: not all the sky is stars, nor is all the sky empty spaces; these latter serve as background to enhance the former, and shadows alternate with light to make it shine the brighter.
>
> However marvellous and superlative the *conceptos* may be, they will fail if ill-starred, for the question of fortune is an irremediable defect. What can I say of fashion? Some

conceptos are in favour at one time and out of it at other times, only to find re-acceptance later on, because there is nothing new under the sun. Allegories were once in vogue, and not so long ago similes were all the fashion. Nowadays mysterious and enigmatic statements hold the field.[61] To think in the manner of the day is as important as to display *ingenio*: my own taste is for pleasing alternation, a varied beauty, for if 'Nature is beautiful because of its excessive variety', that is still more true of Art.[62]

The main Italian theorists of Wit, Matteo Peregrini (c. 1595–1652) and Emanuele Tesauro (1592–1675), write a more lucid and engaging style and their treatises are more systematically developed, but they lack Gracián's brilliance, nervous agility and critical flair, and their works cannot compare as anthologies of Wit with his. Their aims and approach are basically the same. Writing before Gracián, Peregrini has a simpler terminology. *Ingegno*, which is the intellectual capacity for Wit, produces *acutezza*, which is the conceit, *concetto* being a synonym. The aim of Wit is the marvellous (which includes the element of surprise); this consists in finding an *artificioso* link between ideas or things. The link, *ligamento*, is Gracián's 'correspondence'.

Tesauro, writing after Gracián, has the same terminology as the latter: *ingegno* (the creative artistic imagination), operating through *argutezza* (Wit) produces the *concetto* (conceit) by means of a *ligamento* uniting its two terms. But Tesauro uses 'metaphor' as a synonym for conceit, and clearly states, what Gracián seeks to avoid, that all conceits are metaphors; but they are metaphors of a special kind, in which the more remote the terms the better the conceit. The title of his work, *The Aristotelian Telescope*, indicates his starting-point in that philosopher's definition of metaphor, whose ramifications the work explores. The characteristic element of a conceit is thus explicitly, for Tesauro, a question of degree; whereas Gracián never wavered in insisting to the end, despite the fact that a clear-cut definition eluded him, that *conceptos* moved on a higher level than, or in a different dimension from, the figures of rhetoric—a dimension of intellectual artistry.

This points to a basic difference between Gracián and Tesauro, the former is more intellectual, the latter more poetic. For Tesauro, *ingegno* possesses not only the power of 'perspicacity' but also that of 'versatility' (*versabilità* [*sic*]): while the former penetrates all the 'circumstances' that condition or surround objects, the latter sees their relationships

> and with marvellous skill puts the one in the place of the other, like conjurers their tricks. And this is metaphor, the mother of poems, of symbols and of emblems. And that man is more *ingegnoso* who can recognize and link more remote circumstances.[63]

> Here we have arrived at last, step by step, at the topmost summit of the figures of *ingegno*, compared with which all the other figures paraded so far are of little value, metaphor being the most *ingegnoso* and acute, the rarest and most marvellous, the most pleasurable and useful, the most eloquent and fruitful offspring of the human intellect.[64]

Tesauro is most poetic when he points to the 'symbolical subtleties' (*simboliche arguzie*) of Nature, who shows herself so wise in everything needful for human life, and so subtle and humorous, for no other reason than to show off her ingenuity, in all things that are purely pleasurable. Witness the multitudinous shapes, textures, structures and colours of flowers. Some are suitable for adorning the helmet of Bellona, others the tresses of Venus; some are appropriate for graves, others for altars (innate correspondences, so to speak). Flowers are such that the rising sun wishes to make a heaven of earth by seeming to scatter on it the stars from the sky. Flowers are nature's innumerable witticisms: she jests and speaks with thousands of subtle and ingenious conceits.[65] A man who could write in this vein would have been receptive to an aspect of Góngora's nature poetry, especially in the *Soledades*, that the more intellectual Gracián probably did not appreciate. Gracián delighted in witticisms and sharp repartee, but Tesauro makes us aware of another side to seventeenth-century Wit—the response to the whimsical ingenuities of nature.[66]

Góngora is not blind to nature's fancies. The crest of the cock ('the singing herald of the sun') is dentate like a crown, but since it is not golden (or stiff) it is a purple turban, (as befits the minister of a potentate from the Orient), below which there hangs a coral beard:

> doméstico es del Sol nuncio canoro,

y—de coral barbado—no de oro
ciñe, sino de púrpura turbante.[67]

In *Polifemo*, the objects of nature are put to fanciful uses. The
Cyclops imagines the nymphs, Galatea and her companions,
weaving dance measures on the sea-bed to the harsh accompani-
ment of the clacking of clams—a dissonant sound, but the only
castanets available in the ocean:

o al disonante número de almejas
—marino, si agradable no, instrumento—
coros tejiendo estés, escucha un día
mi voz, por dulce, cuando no por mía. (381–4)

The conclusion of this stanza ('listen one day to my voice because
of its sweetness, not because it is mine') points to a continuous
humorous element in the poem—the ugly giant's naive confidence
in his attractiveness. Humour, of course, runs through all the
hyperbolical descriptions of his appearance and activities; such as
his 'torrential beard', 'cascading down his breast, furrowed too
late, or badly, or in vain, by the fingers of his hand':

Su pecho inunda, o tarde, o mal, o en vano
surcada aun de los dedos de su mano. (63–4)

The last line of Cunningham's translation is a happy rendering of
the humorous conceit:

Flooding his breast, and barbered, late or ill,
By a prodigious hand with puny skill.

Though all the conceits of *Polifemo* are to be taken seriously as
imaginative correspondences, they should not all be taken
solemnly. The pale-faced guardian, gilding the pear, which was
noticed above (p.41), is more funny, perhaps malicious, than
solemn. A not dissimilar conceit is the 'hypocritical apple' (83):
this is hypocritical because it deceives, not by pallor (like the
wan-faced religious penitents parading their mortifications), but
by its ruddiness (since a bite reveals that a red apple can still be
sour). Such humour adds an agreeable element of surprise, and
therefore of Wit, to the poetic splendour of the imagery.

The first line of stanza 43 is a joke that some commentators have
not missed. Góngora has just united Acis and Galatea in their
embrace. At this point the reader who knew his Ovid would
expect Polyphemus to start his song; and even the reader who
did not know his Ovid would expect the next line 'Su aliento

humo, sus relinchos fuego' (337) [His breath smoke, his neighing fire] to herald the re-appearance of Polyphemus, but all such readers should be amused to find themselves put off by a 'false start', for Góngora is beginning a description of the sunset, through the entrance of the sun horse, Aethon.

6. Polifemo : *Analysis and Interpretation*

The foregoing partial study of the imagery of *Polifemo* in the light of *Agudeza y arte de ingenio* has not been intended to convert anyone who finds Gracián's theory of poetry misguided, if not indeed repellent. The aim has been to suggest that such a theory is not irrelevant to what Góngora wrote and how he wrote it; that, in fact, such a study adds very considerably to the understanding of the poem's form and structure within its epoch.[68] One can accept this as true without thereby enjoying the poem any less. It may, of course, make one enjoy the poem anew or in a different way; on the other hand it may make one reject the poem after previously accepting it. Acceptance or rejection is a matter of personal taste or judgement, depending on what the poem communicates to us on our terms. The attempt to understand the best art forms of a period on their own terms should be an interesting, perhaps rewarding, historical experience which may well strengthen and deepen our first response; if it does not, this may be detrimental to our knowledge of the history of literature, but it need not affect our enjoyment of individual works. I must not be understood as upholding the legitimacy of giving any meaning one wants to poetry before the symbolists. It does not need much acumen to realize that for earlier periods the so-called 'intentional fallacy' is more likely than not to be itself fallacious. But it is, of course, true that no great seventeenth-century poem will move every reader in the same way, and will not therefore 'mean' the same thing.

The preceding study emphasized that awareness of the *conceptista* structure of *Polifemo* has in no way to weaken or tarnish an awareness of its sensuousness. 'Vagas cortinas de volantes vanos' (213) is felt to be sensuous poetry long before it is recognized to be a subtle conceit. This will be constantly emphasized anew in the analysis that now follows. Many readers may prefer to stop there—at the melodiousness of the sound pattern, at the neatness of the syntactical structure and at the sense impression that results. When the revaluation of 'Gongorism' began in the third decade of our century, this was the poetic value that was stressed. Gerald Brenan, whose *Literature of the Spanish People* was the work of a sensitive reader of poetry, which manuals of that kind rarely are, found that the story of *Polifemo* 'has little importance':

> the effect arrived at is not so much that of a series of poetic incidents as of a continuous atmosphere in which objects melt and fuse into one another. This atmosphere is that of summer, so that the impression one gets from reading it resembles a confused, half-sleepy recollection of the sun-drenched, light-soaked hills and plains of Sicily . . . Góngora made of this poem a texture of light, colour and sonorous language . . .

Góngora has lent himself inevitably to impressionistic criticism, both among academics and non-academics. The first major academic study of the *Soledades* summed up the poem's aesthetic value in these terms:

> Obscurity, no: radiant clarity, dazzling clarity. A clarity of intimate, profound illumination. Shining sea: blue crystal. Sky the colour of sapphire, unblemished, constellated with diamonds, or torn by the curved passage of the sun. *Abbreviated world, renewed and pure*, among the harmonies of white, red and green. A world illuminated not only by the light of day, but by an irradiation, an interior light, like a phosphorecence over everything. *Claritas*. Hyperluminosity. An aesthetic light: clear because beautiful, beautiful because clear.[69]

The first systematic study of Góngora, by Walther Pabst, came to the conclusion that he was a great impressionist, not only because his poetry dealt with sense experience and not with the life of the spirit, but also because it distorted perception by limiting it to the impression produced on the senses only by the surface of objects. Where the memory of mythology does not intervene, and often when it does, Góngora, says Pabst, communicates only the impression an object makes upon him without bothering about its real nature. The majority of his metaphors are due to this obsession ('Manie'). He willingly allows himself to be deceived by the senses, believing everything they tell him. His world is so splendidly colourful because in it everything is what it seems: amber *can* be distilled and the sun's rays *can* be spun.[70]

This, for Pabst, is the essence of Góngora's art, and the conclusion this leads to is that he is ingenuous:

> Góngora is much more ingenuous than other men, above all much more ingenuous than his readers. For who on earth is more ingenuous than an impressionist? The impressionist is the man who has returned to the sensibility of the child. Spain has no greater impressionist than Góngora . . . no-one has practised impressionism with such consistency or with such sensuous candour. When his senses receive nourishment they rob it of perspective.[71]

Having understood why Góngora was admired for being an *ingenio* we find him three centuries later admired for being an *ingénu*. This complete contradiction perhaps illustrates, in the history of criticism, what has been called the 'dissociation of sensibility' in the history of poetry. The critic can no longer recognize a sensibility unified through the integration of thought and feeling. After the passage just quoted Pabst lists a selection of impressionist details that make up the 'mosaic' of *Polifemo*. Each one of these we recognize as a concept formed by a correspondence between two material objects, which is important either for the particular context or for the conceptual pattern of the poem as a whole. The first of these impressionistic details—Góngora naively believing what his senses tell him—is the mountain that is either a 'vault' or a 'tomb'. But how, we may ask, can a mountain look like either? A dome, yes; but not a vault, and certainly not a tomb. The fact, of course, is that Góngora's senses told him no such thing; what his mind conceived was much more specific: that Mount Etna was 'either the vault of Vulcan's forge, or the tomb of the bones of Typhon' (lines 27–8). No impressionism here, but a correlation of Fire and Death right at the start of this poem on Love and Jealousy. Examples from Pabst of 'impressionist details' that have already been discussed here as conceits, are the 'unshorn meadow', and the 'combed garden'. How can one have a sense impression of either? Of an *unmown* meadow, and of a *cultivated* garden, yes; these would derive from sense impressions, but not the images Góngora actually thought out. Such analysis is too simplist even to explain itself.

The Góngora New Criticism, sketched in Dámaso Alonso's 1927 edition of *Soledades*, was given body by his scholarly study of the poet's *culto* vocabulary and syntax, *La lengua poética de Góngora* (Madrid 1935), and finally came to full flower in his masterly study of *Polifemo*.[72] 'How disappointed (said Alonso) would Paul Verlaine and the French symbolists and our modernists have been, if they could have known the logical laws and the tightly organized structure of the Gongorine system! No unruly abandon, no nebulosity, no impressionism, an implacable rigour, an exquisite order.'[73] But these are logic, rigour and order at the service of art. Alonso's method of stylistic analysis succeeded in elucidating the manifold subtle ways in which Góngora's manipulation of the melodic and rhythmic resources of the *ottava rima*— the creation of expressive sound patterns evoking emotions or moods—his syntactical elaborations and even his *culto* vocabulary, are all constituent parts of the form (the 'signifier') that communicates the complex sense (the 'signified') of the poem.

This is a splendid example of scholarship at the service of literary criticism; but though it has exhaustively explained Góngora's *culteranismo* it has stopped short of his *conceptismo*, because it is an analysis based on an aesthetic that does not appreciate, and consequently ignores, Gracián's 'Art of the Mind'. The sensuous dimension continues to dominate the critic's field of vision even though the sensations are no longer nebulous. Now clearly described and accounted for, the sensations fall into two groups: darkness and monstrosity; light and beauty. Alonso sees the form of the poem as musical, with two subjects, Polyphemus (darkness) and Galatea (light), alternating throughout the poem and re-appearing with variations on each occasion.

The Light-Beauty subject is the exaltation of the beauty of woman and of human love within the tradition, which it brings to culmination, of the sixteenth century, the Age of Petrarchism; this is a spirit of serenity. The Darkness-Monstrosity subject is the new baroque age, threatening the achieved harmonies of the Renaissance; this is a spirit of violence. The contrast and interplay of the two subjects represents the pulsating life-giving forces of nature within the destructive energy she can also unleash.

Beauty is threatened, as it were, by a tremendous earthquake or a ferocious hurricane. With monstrosity and violence go the insistence on the exuberance and prolific abundance of nature, her over-richness, her over-productive vitality. Beneath the surface of the achieved harmony of the poetic form, there beat the elemental earth forces in association with the voluptuousness of love.

The serene and the tormented; the luminous and the gloomy; softness and roughness; gracefulness, aloofness and terrible repressed desires. The eternal feminine and the eternal masculine, which constitute all the counterpoint, the tension, the *chiaroscuro* of the Baroque. In one work of Góngora's they became condensed in such a way that the work, in itself, is an epitome of all that age's complexity and of everything that was fermenting within it. Yes, they—light and dark, law and violence, grace and ill-omen—became condensed in the *Fable of Polyphemus*, which is, for that reason, the most representative work of the European Baroque.

But the astonishing thing is this: Galatea and Polyphemus (the heavenly and the earthy) find their resolution—aesthetically—in a single organism: in that *Fable of Polyphemus and Galatea* where they are now one in an eternal creation of art. Prodigy of art.[74]

The beauty-monstrosity polarity has been minimized by later critics, who have tended to stress either the pagan eroticism of the poem or its naturalistic vision of life. Robert Jammes finds the key to the poem's interpretation in what Góngora added to Ovid— the central passage describing the fulfilment of the love of Acis and Galatea. The poem represents the triumph of Love, 'of a pagan Love with all the sensuality and freedom implied in that term'. Not only a triumph over Galatea but also over Polyphemus, whom it humanizes and civilizes. It was not possible for Góngora to alter the ending, but Jammes finds it worthy of note that while Ovid makes the Cyclops, in his song to Galatea, threaten to kill Acis, Góngora removes any note of premeditation from the act, which thus becomes the result of an impulsive surge of jealousy that makes the giant human. It is noteworthy, also, that the description of the death of Acis is reduced to the minimum and his metamorphosis rendered instantaneous, so that the river reaching the sea strikes at the end the note of victory—a triumph, however sorrowful, of Love over death.[75]

Góngora departs from Ovid in not putting the story into Galatea's mouth; he cannot therefore repeat the tears with which Ovid makes her tell it. None-the-less, to read the triumph of Love over death into Góngora's version seems wishful thinking on the part of a critic who would make of the poet a pagan sensualist untouched by disillusion. The triumphal aspect of the ending had been earlier stressed by R.O.Jones, who was on surer ground in seeing it rather as the triumph of Life over death. 'It is a poem on the brevity of happiness, but . . . it is not a pessimistic work. The emphasis throughout is on life and beauty.' Though discord shatters the harmony achieved by Acis and Galatea, the discord is resolved:

Acis is changed into a stream, beautiful in itself and a cause of beauty, but his reception in the arms of the sea culminates in what is distinctly a note of triumph. . . . This, then, is a story in which, though death enters, vitality prevails. . . . Góngora seems to move in a poetic atmosphere of optimism in which death is absorbed into the invincible harmony of the universe. For the Neoplatonist, the universe is wholly good; but the very abundance of created things leads inevitably to conflict between some of them. These apparent discords—violence, the preying of animals one on another, death, decay—are in reality only parts of a larger concert. Plotinus, a great influence on Renaissance thought, put it thus: 'Besides, these accidents are not without their service in the co-ordination and completion of the Universal system. One thing perishes, and the Cosmic Reason—whose control nothing anywhere eludes—employs that ending to the beginning of something new.'[76]

Joining issue with Jones on the alleged Neoplatonism of *Polifemo*, Colin Smith saw Góngora's Nature as less harmonious, more elemental and primitive:

The idea of evil is, in fact, necessary to complete the picture of Nature, for no amount of mere prettiness would satisfy us. The idea of violence and death is the last link in the chain of life. There is not merely a visual oneness about Góngora's

Nature, but a logic in its functioning which conveys a sense of almost Darwinian completeness. The origins of life are not known scientifically but are explained in fragile fictions, which can then be further glossed in a poetic way exactly suited to Góngora's art. . . . The human and semi-human beings emerge from the sea, a rich source of life and perhaps the origin of all life, as biologists suggest. Once the cast is assembled, whatever its origins, the situation is Darwinian enough. Polyphemus kills the wild beast, for clothing; the wolf kills the sheep, for food; and Polyphemus kills Acis, his competitor in love. Being preys on being and the strongest survive. . . .

On the spiritual side too it is difficult to make out a case for Góngora's Neoplatonism. Man in the *Polifemo* seems to have few spiritual needs and fewer observances. The Graeco-Roman gods are present, in metaphor at least; they are not worshipped, although they are invoked finally to secure Acis' transformation. . . . Galathea is a fertility-figure whose un-formalized worship is partly erotic, partly spiritual. For the rest, the countryside is peopled with divinities which represent the forces of creation, generation and growth, a diversity of animistic or pantheistic forces wholly incompatible with Neoplatonism. . . .

In conclusion, I repeat that the *Polifemo* should be presented to readers not as a mere archaic myth or as a brilliant piece of *poésie pure*, but as a poem about the world of Nature and man's place in it. In it Góngora refused to take an easy, simplist view, or indeed to propound any single philosophy. All we can say is that to him, as surely still to us, Nature is difficult, multifarious and anarchical, full of warring elements (among them the humans), possibly created and still evolving, lacking a grand design although possessing a sort of Darwinian completeness; always fascinating and always beautiful.[77]

One may wonder whether the desire, in these interpretations, to find philosophical ideas in *Polifemo* is not misplaced. Góngora's recreation of the myth certainly suggests a 'view of life', or at least of certain enduring aspects of it, but it seems misguided to look for ideas that can be allied to a philosophy tenable in terms of his own age. Both Jones and Smith stress, as others have also done, that the *Polifemo* represents an 'amoral cosmos', that neither in it nor in the *Soledades*, is there any suggestion of theistic or Christian thinking; in consequence the need is felt to fill these gaps. But morality and Christian theology are not present in the *Polifemo* because they are irrelevant. In both his major poems Góngora is refashioning in his own special way the Renaissance literary tradition of Pastoral, which represents a nostalgia for a humanistic, not a theological, state of innocence (there being no contradiction between the two, since the plane of nature is distinct from the plane of grace and its positive values can be praised in their own right). In *Polifemo*, however, Pastoral takes the form of the recreation of the Golden Age, the classical myth of the first stage of the world's history: neither Góngora nor his readers would forget that this stage was not only pre-Christian but also pre-Judaic, and therefore pre-theological. Góngora's conception of this primitive age may well show analogies with later Darwinism, but one is scarcely justified in seeing it as the view of Nature that Góngora had formulated in 1613 from his reading and from his thinking on his own experience.[78]

Alonso's tension between beauty and monstrosity, serenity and violence, fecundity and destructiveness; Jammes's triumph of a pagan Love; Jones's resolution of discord in the triumph of life over death; Smith's Nature, complete and beautiful in the anarchy of its warring elements: all these are valid readings of *Polifemo*, each within its particular focus, the differences between them being differing criteria of thematic significance and variations of emphasis. To seek for the poetic unity of the work through concentration on the Wit of its metaphorical patterns, as will now be attempted here, provides another focus. The emphasis will lie in the way the basic 'correspondences' of the poem build up image complexes that are significantly interrelated—forming, in other words, a system of organic conceits. Gracián called *Polifemo* a 'polished, eloquent and recondite' poem.[79] Alonso's commentary has shown how well chosen were these adjectives of praise, but perhaps something more may yet be said to bring out the special nuance of *agudeza* in the quality of reconditeness.

The source of the poem, as has already been stated, is Ovid's *Metamorphoses*, Book XIII, lines 724–897. The original Latin, with an English translation and notes on the passage by David West, are included in this volume as section v. As Dámaso Alonso has shown,[80] Góngora was not influenced by any other classical author or by any of his Italian and Spanish predecessors in the reworking of the mythological fable, but went direct to Ovid. In the course of his analysis of *Polifemo* Robert Jammes compares Góngora's version of the story with Ovid's and discusses the changes he introduces and the resulting differences of tone and emphasis.[81] The story is differently conceived. In Ovid the emphasis is entirely on Polyphemus; Acis and Galatea are scarcely described and their love is merely referred to as an accomplished fact. The giant's song takes up exactly half of Ovid's narrative; in Góngora it constitutes only one-fifth of the poem, which is divided almost equally between Polyphemus (lines 25–96, 337–472) on the one hand, and Galatea (97–192, 217–88) and Acis (193–216, 289–304) on the other, with a short closing section (437–504) in which the three are brought together. Whereas in Ovid there is only one thematic motif, in Góngora there are two; and in one he develops what Ovid ignores—Acis's successful wooing of Galatea (305–36). In Ovid the sole emphasis is on the pathos of unrequited love and the tragic effects of jealousy, but Góngora offsets this by an equal emphasis on the positive aspect of love.

Sicily is a pastoral setting for the poem, an island flowing in milk and honey, abundant in flocks and fruits. What are now called the literary archetypes of Garden and Shepherd, which had been given their enduring classical form in Virgil's *Eclogues*, were rediscovered early in the sixteenth century in Sannazaro's *Arcadia*, to become one of the most characteristic modes of Renaissance literature, a nostalgic withdrawal from the harsh world of reality into an ideal environment in which men and women could be imagined living free from ambition and the lust for power; in particular, an environment in which it was possible to portray human love free from any suggestion of lascivious grossness.[82] In Góngora's poetry it is only in a pastoral setting that sexual love can be described or suggested as wholesome and innocent; in other modes, notably the satiric, it is invariably venal or adulterous.

The Sicily of *Polifemo* is not, however, a Renaissance Arcadia, such as was to be found (in Spain) in the novels of Montemayor and Gil Polo, in Cervantes's *Galatea*, Lope de Vega's *Arcadia* and in countless poems. Colin Smith has stressed the difference between Arcadia and this Sicily. Pastoral activities (sheep, goats, milking, shearing) and traditional pastoral images (elms and vines) are only minor and incidental elements in the poem. So too are navigation and trade, which receive anomalous mention in Polyphemus's song. There are no houses, no temples, no cities. The most striking difference is that Galatea and Acis go unclothed, and that their love has an 'animal' quality. In the *Soledades*, by contrast, there is a pastoral society, 'economically simple but morally rich, and old men speak eloquently with a far from primitive wisdom ... [the shepherds] do not simply mate in the woods, but are married according to elaborate rites in which Society participates; and the land is free of giants.'

In Renaissance pastoral, whether in verse or in prose, Nature is consistently present, but more as a background against which courtly love-affairs are carried on in a relaxed and rather puritanical way. In the *Polifemo* Nature occupies the whole canvas and the human figures move about in the picture dwarfed by trees, mountains, sky and stars, just as they are dwarfed in Mazo's painting. Whereas in pastoral our gaze is typically limited to a pleasantly landscaped setting having a few conventional elements—stream, willows, shade —in the *Polifemo* the vistas opened up are infinite ... [All these differences throw] into relief the starkness and primitiveness of the *Polifemo*, in which the processes of landscape-formation and species-creation are still going on, and in which the gods still walk the earth.[83]

The reason for these differences, however, is that Góngora is going back to an older tradition than that of Renaissance Pastoral, one that is Medieval as well as classical, the myth of the Golden Age under the rule of Saturn, before men tilled the soil and built houses for shelter. The *locus classicus* of the myth is in Hesiod, but Virgil gave it a new orientation and Ovid crystallized it into a *topos* in the opening of the *Metamorphoses*. Human love, however, was absent from the myth, until the Middle Ages introduced it, in a free and unembarrassed form, in Jean de Meun's continuation of the *Roman de la rose*.[84] Whereas the *Soledades*, like most of

Renaissance pastoral, is a restoration of an imaginative idyllic, but civilized, existence, the *Polifemo* is entirely mythic, although the purist can find some anachronisms if he is so minded. The one disparity (fundamental, of course, to the fable) is Polyphemus's jealous killing of Acis, an act of violence befitting the Third, or Brazen, Age. This apart, Góngora's Sicily is the compendium of the beneficent and fertile nature that marked the reign of Saturn, providing everything that human life requires, with plains rich in corn, and with mountains rich in flocks and in trees that bear in abundance every fruit that man gathers. Góngora lavishes more details on the description of his island, with which the poem opens, than had any of his predecessors in the telling of the fable, including Ovid. No aspect of nature is missing, for Sicily is surrounded by the sea, whose waves continually fall on the rocks and sands of its shores; the sea is, in fact, an important motif. A more dominant feature than the sea, however, is Mount Etna. Although Góngora selects Cape Lilybaeum (now Boeo), the western promontory of the island where Marsala is situated, as the site of Polyphemus's cavern, his description of the locality associates the Cape with this volcano despite the fact that it is at the eastern end of the island. Here are found the first of the correspondences on which the imagery of the poem turns. Through his characteristic 'either-or' construction, Etna becomes both the vault over a forge and a tomb. The correspondence is provided by mythology, for the fire of Etna was explained by placing Vulcan's forge within it, and its huge mass accounted for by making it the tomb of the giant Typhoeus or Typhon, who made war against heaven and was crushed under the rock hurled by Jupiter.

> Donde espumoso el mar siciliano
> el pie argenta de plata al Lilibeo
> (bóveda o de las fraguas de Vulcano,
> o tumba de los huesos de Tifeo),
> pálidas señas cenizoso un llano
> —cuando no del sacrílego deseo—
> del duro oficio da. (25–31)
> [Where, as it treads on the Sicilian surge,
> Marsala's foot is shod with silver foam
> (Either a vault that houses Vulcan's forge,

Or serves the bones of Typhon for a tomb)
Upon an ashy plain pale signs emerge
From this one's sacrilegious wish, or from
    The other's toil.]

This is a circumlocution, characteristic of Góngora, of the type that Dámaso Alonso has called 'elusion' because it eludes the simple description or naming of an object; here Etna itself is never mentioned. If it is only a question of circumlocution this could properly be called tiresome pedantry in most cases. But generally these mythological allusions provide or confirm significant correspondences. They represent what Gracián called 'the Wit of erudition' (Disc. lviii and lix), whose effectiveness he said, lies in its 'application' (i.e. the way one term of the correspondence is applied to the other), in this case how the forge of Vulcan and the tomb of Typhoeus apply to the cavern of Polyphemus, to which the circumlocution is being directed. The application lies in the ideas suggested by the correspondences,[85] namely fire and death. Their 'geographical' fusion makes them different aspects of the same thing; they are, for the poet, related concepts that merge into one and become associated with the setting of the story, and especially with the Cyclops, the site of whose cavern is being described in these terms. Fire was a traditional symbol for passion and love, and burning was the commonest image for the stress of love in the Petrarchan poetic tradition. The fire of Etna dies out in the lava ash that covers the plain. *Cinis*, or its plural *cineres*, were frequently used in Latin for the ashes of a cremated corpse, for a dead body or even death itself. Its Spanish derivative *ceniza*, from which *ceniciento* was formed, also had this connotation.[86] The word *pálido* likewise carried strong associations with Death. In Latin the adjective was frequently used of the Lower World, which Lucan called the *pallida regna* of Dis. Horace's lines on 'Pale Death' the leveller are well-known:

pallida Mors aequo pulsat pede pauperum tabernas
regumque turres.[87]

The Spanish *pálido* was a loan-word from Latin, which according to Vilanova is first found recorded in 1584.[88] It naturally brought with it the associations of the original and is frequently found connected with death in seventeenth-century literature.[89] 'Pálidas señas cenizoso un llano' thus reinforces the idea of death in *tumba de los huesos*. Góngora was not following tradition in describing the site of Polyphemus's cavern in these terms: he did not find this description in Ovid or in any other source. In consequence he is interconnecting love and death at the very start of the poem; they will be interconnected at the end. The application of these two concepts to Polyphemus is clear: he will feel the fire of love, but his love will be death-dealing, not life-giving.

On the other hand, the association of Sicily with Vulcan and the tomb of Tiphoeus is common enough in Latin poetry, and in Italian and Spanish poetry prior to, and contemporaneous with, Góngora,[90] to make these two lines in isolation a commonplace. To see them as 'Wit of erudition' is justifiable only if the fire symbol and the concept of death form part of image-complexes organically related to the developing theme. This is indeed the case, for Góngora invariably puts traditional elements to original uses. The associations of death are first developed as we move from the site of Polyphemus's cavern to the cavern itself, which is described in terms of darkness:

caliginoso lecho, el seno obscuro
ser de la negra noche nos lo enseña
infame turba de nocturnas aves,
gimiendo tristes y volando graves.

(Literally: 'An infamous flock of night birds, hooting mournfully and flying ponderously, shows us that the caliginous bed is the dark womb of black night'.) No translation could ever capture the overwhelming impression of ominous darkness and inky blackness conveyed by the original. This is Góngora at his most impressionistic. Dámaso Alonso has analysed the *sensation* of darkness, finding its causes in the choice of words, the relation of vowel sounds and the rhythmical structure; in, for instance the marvellous line 'infame T U R ba de noc T U R nas aves' with its two main stresses symmetrically placed on the same phonetically 'dark' syllable, the fourth and the eighth, with three syllables preceding the first *tur*, three syllables between the two, and three after the second *tur*.[91]

From the standpoint of Wit, however, what needs analysis and explanation is the *concept* of darkness. It becomes clear in the conceit that opens stanza 8, when the image of blackness is transferred from the cavern to Polyphemus himself and associated with death: his hair, wavy and streaming, resembles a river, and being black, it resembles the dark waters of Lethe:

Negro el cabello, imitador undoso
de las obscuras aguas del Leteo,
al viento que lo peina proceloso,
vuela sin orden, pende sin aseo;
un torrente es su barba impetüoso,
que (adusto hijo de este Pirineo)
su pecho inunda, o tarde, o mal, o en vano
surcada aun de los dedos de su mano. (57–64)
[His hair, which curls in raven tresses, seems
To rival Lethe's dark obscurities;
Unkempt it hangs or in disorder streams
Under the comb of the tempestuous breeze;
His beard like an impetuous torrent teems,
Swarthy as fits its parent Pyrenees,
Flooding his breast, and barbered, late or ill,
By a prodigious hand with puny skill.]

The associations of 'pálidas señas cenizoso un llano' have thus become explicit in the first major image-complex of the poem: darkness—night—blackness—death. This is accompanied by imagery of violence and disorder. The giant's beard is 'a tempestuous torrent' that 'floods' his breast; since the only comb his hair knows is the stormy wind, it is blown about in disorder.[92] Developing what is no more than a hint in Ovid, Góngora carries this correspondence further when he equates the music that Polyphemus plays on his pipe with nature's destructive storms:

La selva se confunde, el mar se altera,
rompe Tritón su caracol torcido,
sordo huye el bajel a velo y remo:
¡tal la música es de Polifemo! (93–6)
[The tree-tops toss, the surges crash and grind,
His trump of twisted nacre Triton breaks,
Fear wings with sail or oar the deafened boats:
So barbarous are Polyphemus' notes!]

When the giant later sings his song, 'the thunder of his voice struck with lightning the caves and the shores already warned by the barbarous pipe':

> Las cavernas en tanto, los ribazos
> que ha prevenido la zampoña ruda,
> el trueno de la voz fulminó luego   (357–9)

This correspondence indicates that Polyphemus is more than a character in a fable: he is akin to one of the forces of nature:

Though the Cyclops rules the island materially because of his size and strength, spiritually it is ruled by Galatea, who is the deity all its inhabitants worship. Her description gives us the second, and a contrasting, image-complex, that of whiteness and light. To use the terminology of Northrop Frye, while the imagery surrounding Polyphemus is 'demonic', that for Galatea is 'apocalyptic'.

> Ninfa, de Doris hija, la más bella,
> adora, que vio el reino de la espuma.
> Galatea es su nombre, y dulce en ella
> el terno Venus de sus Gracias suma.
> Son una y otra luminosa estrella
> lucientes ojos de su blanca pluma:
> si roca de cristal no es de Neptuno,
> pavón de Venus es, cisne de Juno.   (97–104)
> [He loves a nymph, daughter of Doris, fair
> Above all seen in Ocean's kingdom yet;
> Her name is Galatea, and in her
> Of Venus' Graces all the charms are met.
> Bright stars, both one and other, are the pair
> Of shining eyes in snow-white plumage set:
> If not a rock of crystal in the sea,
> Then Juno's swan or Venus' peacock she.]

This conceit has already been quoted above (pp. 24–5) as an example of the 'mystery' that Gracián considered an essential element in Wit. Galatea's eyes have the radiance of the eyes on a peacock's tail feathers, but since they are set in the whiteness of her face they are peacock's eyes set in a swan's white down. In addition to having a skin with the beautiful translucency of crystal, she has all the loveliness of the swan (which is the attribute of Venus) and the splendid beauty of the peacock (which is the attribute of Juno); but by a 'conceit of disparity' Góngora inverts the birds and calls her Juno's swan and Venus's peacock. Dámaso Alonso sees this inversion as a device to fuse the two birds into one: Galatea is a swan that is a peacock and a peacock that is a swan. This is thus a composite sensuous image, fusing together the different aspects of a woman's beauty.[93] The conceit, however, does not fuse together the two birds but the two goddesses: it makes Venus Juno by giving her the peacock, and Juno Venus by transferring to her the swan. The purpose of the mythological allusions is to endow Galatea with the beauty of Venus and the majesty of Juno. Why not, then, simply say 'cisne de Venus es, pavón de Juno'? Because Venus and Juno were rivals (as the *Aeneid* tells us); they had been so ever since the former triumphed in the Judgement of Paris. Venus had promised him the most beautiful woman on earth, while Juno had promised him power. Love and power compete in human life as rival promoters of happiness, but Góngora resolves the rivalry by merging the two goddesses into a harmony. Galatea, as the universal object of desire, is the principle of concord in human life; in love the beauty of life is possessed and its power and majesty realized: love unifies and harmonizes. Galatea is the only goddess of the island, the only being to whom all the inhabitants offer the sacrifice of their devotion. Galatea is Venus's peacock and Juno's swan, because she overcomes the disharmony in nature; she is beauty and power in one.

White remains the image for Galatea's beauty throughout the poem: her limbs are 'snow' (lines 180, 483) and the flowers that are the metaphors for her form are white, jasmine (179) and lilies (220). But her lips are red; later, when 'sucked' by Acis, they are given the rich red of carnations (331–2). So to the imagery of light and whiteness with which Galatea is initially presented, there is straightaway added red, and with it a third divinity is associated with her, the god of Love:

Purpúreas rosas sobre Galatea
la Alba entre lilios cándidos deshoja:
duda el Amor cuál más su color sea,
o púrpura nevada, o nieve roja.   (105–8)
[Encrimsoned roses mixed with lilies white
On Galatea's beauty Dawn bestows,
Till Love can hardly tell her hue aright,
Whether a rosy snow or snowy rose.]

The red rose, a flower sacred to Venus, was a traditional symbol of love; it owed its colour to the goddess's blood when, plucking roses (then only white), she pricked her finger on the thorns and stained the flowers red. This fable produces the 'conceit of dissonance'—white that is red, or red that is white—whereby beauty and love are rendered inseparable: beauty is lovable, a loved object is beautiful. Polyphemus's tragedy is that he cannot be loved. Galatea, on the other hand, cannot not be loved.

Having thus scattered the petals of red roses over Galatea's white lilies, Góngora then stresses the fact that all the inhabitants of Sicily, all the gods of the surrounding sea, everybody without exception, is in love with Galatea. All either pursue and woo her, or worship her from afar. This is not in Ovid. By adding this to his source Góngora is making Beauty the aspiration of all men, and by associating this love with husbandry (which again is not in Ovid) he also associates it with the creativity of nature, whose crops are white (wool) and red (wine), like Galatea, as well as golden (corn):

> A Pales su viciosa cumbre debe
> lo que a Ceres, y aún mas su vega llana;
> pues si en la una granos de oro llueve,
> copos nieva en la otra mil de lana
> De cuantos siegan oro, esquilan nieve,
> O en pipas guardan la exprimida grana,
> bien sea religión, bien amor sea,
> deidad, aunque sin templo, es Galatea. (145-52)
> [To Pales more her teeming upland owes
> Even than to Ceres her more level plain;
> A thousand woolly snowflakes one bestows
> To match the other's showers of golden grain;
> And all who reap the gold or shear the snows,
> Or purple juice from press to wine-cask strain,
> For love or worship, shrineless though she be,
> Take Galatea for their deity.]

In the preceding stanza Góngora had hyperbolically described the rich fertility of the island. The hyperboles do not make this fertility something monstrous; it is associated with Galatea, not Polyphemus. It is overabundant life, bursting in pastoral richness, and despite the hyperboles, the tone of the lines that express it is serene and harmonious. The produce of this fertility is what the men of the island offer to Galatea, for though she is a deity without a shrine, she is not without her altars. Nature's 'cornucopia' is the offering of love to Beauty:

> Sin aras, no; que el margen donde para
> del espumoso mar su pie ligero,
> al labrador, de sus primicias ara,
> de sus esquilmos es al ganadero;
> de la Copia—a la tierra, poco avara—
> el cuerno vierte el hortelano, entero,
> sobre la mimbre que tejió, prolija,
> si artificiosa no, su honesta hija. (153–60)
> [Shrineless, but yet she has an altar where
> Her light step pauses by the foaming sea,
> On which both herd and ploughman offer her
> The tithes and firstfruits of their industry;
> Grudged nothing by the soil, the gardener
> Empties his horn of plenty liberally
> Into the osier which, though ill designed,
> With no small toil his worthy daughter twined.]

This pastoral sensuousness is the prelude to the erotic sensuousness which Góngora now proceeds to develop as the culmination of this cult of Galatea. The fire imagery, announced in Vulcan's forge, whose hammers beat within the island, now takes the foreground. Just as Etna burns with fire, so too do the young men of Sicily: they are on fire with love for Galatea. In Ovid the fire-love image is applied only to Polyphemus:

> uror enim, laesusque exaestuat acrius ignis,
> cumque suis videor translatam viribus Aetnam
> pectore ferre meo . . . (xiii, 867–9)
> [I burn with love and the more my passion is slighted the more fiercely it boils. The full force of the volcano seems to have left Etna and settled in my breast]

Góngora applies the image universally:

> Arde la juventud, y los arados
> peinan las tierras que surcaron antes,
> mal conducidos, cuando no arrastrados
> de tardos bueyes, cual su dueño errantes (161–4)
> [Youth is on fire, and while the ploughman's share
> Scratches the soil instead of furrowing,

 Ill-drawn or worse, behind a lazy pair
 Of bullocks, like their master wandering]
But Galatea is elusive and flees from her wooers, who are left,
like Etna, to burn alone. The passion of love, if unfulfilled,
frustrates the order and purpose of life. Not only do the oxen
plough aimlessly, but the flocks wander at will with no shepherd
to control them and the dogs, forgetful like their masters, give no
warning of the night-prowling wolf. Unless the god of Love calls
back the shepherd to his flock, the dog, by its silence and its sleep,
will continue to be as heedless as its master. Only the god of
Love—the life principle in nature—can give passion an aim and
purpose, and enable it to burn without consuming itself (lines
165–76).
 At this point in the poem, Acis is introduced; he too is burning
with the heat, for the summer is at its height. This coincides with
his first sight of Galatea, and the situation is expressed in a series
of complex organic conceits.

 Salamandria del Sol, vestido estrellas,
 latiendo el Can del cielo estaba, cuando
 (polvo el cabello, húmidas centellas,
 si no ardientes aljófares, sudando)
 llegó Acis; y de ambas luces bellas
 dulce Occidente viendo al sueño blando,
 su boca dio, y sus ojos cuanto pudo,
 al sonoro cristal, al cristal mudo. (185–92)
 [The Dog, a solar salamander dressed
 In starry garb, is barking in the skies,
 When, dusty-haired, with sweat that on his breast
 Like humid sparks or burning diamonds lies,
 Comes Acis. As he sees the lovely west
 Of sunset sleep that softly seals her eyes,
 The sounding crystal to his lips he raises,
 And sidelong on the silent crystal gazes.]
The conceits are based on the following correspondences: the
star Sirius is a salamander, the beads of perspiration on Acis's
brow are liquid sparks or (literally) fiery pearls, the stream is
crystal and crystal is Galatea, the crystal being sonorous in the
one case and dumb in the other (two examples of Góngora's
frequent doubling of the 'conceit of disproportion'). The

astronomical circumlocution is not rhetorical padding but has an organic connexion with the theme through the first correspondence, the salamander conveying the concept of burning without being consumed. It is the hottest part of the year—the 'dog days' of July and August—when Sirius, in the constellation of the Great Dog, rises in conjunction with the sun. The image is justified by the context. The young men of the island are on fire with love, and on fire with the heat of summer: they are therefore salamanders.[94] Perspiration glistens in the sunlight and its drops are thus 'pearls'; therefore this is an impressionistic metaphor (the English expression '*beads* of sweat' would add, by coincidence, to the witty correspondence). The metaphor becomes a conceit when the glistening is seen as 'sparks' (struck by the flint of the burning sun), and when the moisture of perspiration becomes the material of sparks, and the fire of the sun that of pearls.

Acis, the salamander, must cool his perspiring face and quench his burning thirst at the stream. When he reaches it he sees Galatea lying beside it. The water he comes to drink is 'sonorous crystal' as it splashes among the stones; the silent Galatea is 'dumb crystal' as she lies asleep. This double conceit makes Galatea and the water the same thing.[95] The fire of life is both the fire of the sun and the fire of passion: the water of the stream cools Acis's mouth, but Galatea is the only cooling water that can temper the fire of love.

While it is certainly true to say, as Colin Smith does, that the love-making of Acis and Galatea, which is to follow, has 'a sort of animal simplicity', one should perhaps guard against pressing such a term too far. When she awakens, Galatea realizes at once that the offering placed beside her was not the gift of a 'lustful satyr'; yet Acis is described as the son of a faun (i.e. of a satyr):[96]

> Era Acis un venablo de Cupido,
> de un fauno, medio hombre, medio fiera,
> en Simetis, hermosa ninfa, habido (193–5)
> [Acis, a shaft from Cupid's bow released
> Whom to a faun, half human and half beast,
> A lovely nymph, by name Simetis, bore]

Though Acis's father was half man and half beast, there is nothing bestial about his wooing of Galatea; on the contrary, it has all the courtesy and respect into which Courtly Love had sought to tame passion. Galatea realizes that this must be a lover of a new kind, and gratitude for the 'civilized' absence of an attempted violation is what leads to the break-down of her (for Góngora's age) very 'civilized' reserve:

> Fruta en mimbres halló, leche exprimida
> en juncos, miel en corcho, mas sin dueño;
> si bien al dueño debe, agradecida,
> su deidad culta, venerado el sueño.
> A la ausencia mil veces ofrecida,
> este de cortesía no pequeño
> indicio la dejó—aunque estatua helada—
> más discursiva y menos alterada.

> No al Cíclope atribuye, no, la ofrenda;
> no a sátiro lascivo, ni a otro feo
> morador de las selvas, cuya rienda
> el sueño aflija, que aflojó el deseo. (225-36)

> [Ownerless fruit, butter and honey stored
> In osier, reeds and cork she sees, and knows
> With pleasure that the owner who adored
> Her deity respected her repose;
> And though by fear a thousand times implored
> To hasty flight, while statue-like she froze,
> These signs of no small courtesy combined
> To ease her terrors and to soothe her mind,

> Such gifts none of the lustful satyr train,
> Nor savage dwellers in the trees could make,
> Nor yet the Cyclops, for their passion's rein,
> Strained by desire, the sight of sleep would break.]

'These signs of no small courtesy' make her curious to know who it was who thus respected her sleep: while men are attracted to love by beauty, women (it was held) would be opened to it by the service rendered to them. It is this that makes Galatea take the next step of allowing her eyes to rest on Acis's manly good looks. She does so as respectfully and courteously as he had looked on her,

> compitiendo
> con el garzón dormido en cortesía
> no sólo para, mas el dulce estruendo

del lento arroyo enmudecer querría.   (265–8)
    [rivalling
In courtesy the sleeping youth, for she
Not only paused, but wished the gentle spring
Might hush for him its murmuring melody.]

The whole of this long prelude to love (lines 193–308), with the final oblique (and therefore more witty) allusion to Acis as the Trojan horse introducing fire into the walled city [lines 295–6]), may be reducible to elemental emotions, but it is not primitive. In the elaborate development of the action, and in the complex Wit of thought and expression (of which some examples have been previously analysed) it is the product of a highly refined culture; the poetic beauty of this section, to which the overworked adjective exquisite can surely be applied, is entirely dependent upon this refinement.

The description of the lovers' retreat (lines 309–20) shows all nature contributing to the setting, since their love fulfils the potential harmony of nature. The trees and the rocks give shade from the burning sun; stream, wind, trees, grass, rocks, flowers and birds come together in a union symbolized by the ivy 'trepando troncos y abrazando piedras' (311–12) (Literally: 'ivy climbing the trunks and embracing the stones'), and by the doves' 'joining the rubies of their two bills': 'juntar de sus dos picos los rubíes' (330) to form the bridal bed of Galatea. Upon this bed the poet asks the flowers of Venus to rain down, all those that grow at Paphos and Cnidus, her two great shrines:

Cuantas produce Pafo, engendra Gnido,
negras violas, blancos alhelíes,
llueven sobre el que Amor quiere que sea
Tálamo de Acis ya y de Galatea.   (333–6)
[More stocks than cover Paphos' fields with white,
More dusky violets than Cnidus bears,
Rain on the place where Love ordains to spread
Acis' and Galatea's bridal bed.]

It should be noted that these flowers are only white and black— white stocks and black violets ('dusky' is not a literal translation). The wild violets or violas known to classical antiquity were purple, yellow and white. The viola is more often pale than dark in Latin poets (as also in Petrarch and his successors), though Virgil, who had called them 'pale' in the Second Eclogue (*pallentes violas*, line 47), calls them 'black' in the Tenth (*et nigrae violae sunt*, line 39).[97] Góngora, like Virgil, may merely be using 'black' for 'dark purple' (as horticulturists do today); but the contrast of black and white in his line is emphatic, and the exclusion of other flowers on the bridal bed, the exclusion, also, of the other colours of violas and stocks, will inevitably make the reader recall the black-white contrast already established in the poem, if he had noted at the time the symbolism of these colours—white, the beauty of Galatea; black, the ugliness of Polyphemus, with its strong suggestion of death. Whether by chance or by design, the repetition of the colour symbolism is very appropriate at this point. Black flowers mingle with white on the bridal bed because, though love unites, though it gives and perpetuates life, it cannot escape death, which divides and destroys.

Immediately after the delicate but intensely sensuous presentation of the harmony of love[98] Góngora makes the sun begin to set. His description of the sun touching the sea on the horizon is another of his circumlocutions for fixing time, but just as organic thematically as the Dog Star salamander:

> Su aliento humo, sus relinchos fuego,
> si bien su freno espumas, ilustraba
> las columnas Etón que erigió el griego,
> do el carro de la luz sus ruedas lava (337–40)
> [When Aethon, panting smoke and neighing flame,
> With foaming bit, was scorching with his ray
> The pillars which Alcides toiled to frame
> Where Phoebus dips his chariot-wheel in spray]

The conceit, once again, is a classical image, there being frequent references in Latin poetry to the Sun-God bathing the horses of his chariot in the sea. It is found in the *Metamorphoses*, though not in the Polyphemus story. Ovid also writes of these horses breathing fire. Phoebus says to Phaëthon:

> nec tibi quadripedes animosos ignibus illis,
> quos in pectore habent, quos ore et naribus efflant,
> in promptu regere est (11, 84–6)
> [Nor is it an easy thing for you to control the steeds, hot with those strong fires which they have within their breasts, which they breathe out from mouth and nostrils.]

Desinet ante dies et in alto Phoebus anhelos
aequore tinguet equos, quam consequar omnis verbis
in species translata novas (xv, 418–20)
[The day will come to an end and Phoebus will bathe his
panting horses in the deep waters of the sea before I tell of
all the things which have assumed new forms.]
Góngora recalls the two separate images and brings them to-
gether because the setting sun is a sign that prepares for the death
of Acis. He would not have done so if the details of the elaborate
double image did not have a strict relevance to the symbols and
image-pattern of his poem. The horse breathing smoke and neigh-
ing fire recalls the volcano that presides over the scene of nature's
fertility and of human love, and that is itself symbolical of life and
death; but the primary significance of the image is that the fire,
and with it the light of day, will, like Acis, be extinguished in the
sea. We may ask whether the sea is not beginning to appear as the
symbol of death.

The song of the Cyclops, which now follows, might seem dis-
proportionate in length to all that has preceded, since it in no way
furthers the story. It should be noted, however, that its thirteen
stanzas (lines 361–464) balance the fifteen (lines 193–312) of
the prelude to the lovers' union. The one is the successful wooing
of Galatea, the other represents an unsuccessful and frustrating
wooing of the same nymph. In the theme there is therefore an
appropriate proportion between the two contrasting motifs of
requited and unrequited love.

The extinction of love in death, poetically prepared by the fire-
horse sinking into the sea, is also portended by the contrast be-
tween the harmonious cooing of the doves, which was the
accompaniment to the fulfilment of love, and the music that
Polyphemus plays on his pipes as the sun begins to set, which is
the accompaniment to his unfulfilled love. 'The thunder of his
voice' (359) terrifies Galatea, who is 'muerta de amor, y de temor
no viva' (352). (Literally: 'dead with love, and not alive with
fear'—another double 'conceit of disproportion'.) 'To die of love'
was a tritely commonplace figure; Góngora gives it significance
and reality: the clinging vine will be severed when the elm is
felled (351–6).

The voice of the Cyclops is *horrenda* (465), horrible and

terrifying, but the song he sings contains some of the loveliest verses in the poem: it is tender, pathetic and moving. Góngora is following Ovid in this, but the latter makes the song tender and pathetic because therein he sees the significance of the myth:

> quanta potentia regni
> est, Venus alma, tui! (XIII, 758–9)
> [O kindly Venus, what sovereign power is yours!]

Love holds sway even over a monster, taming his savagery, making him gentle, merciful and anxious to please. This, too, is in Góngora, whose version of the song follows the same sequence of ideas: praise of Galatea's beauty and the complaint of her unresponsiveness; his claims on her love through his pastoral wealth, through his physical attractions and through his now kindly nature; and finally the gift he offers. In Ovid the gift is unusual, 'not easy to come by'—a pair of bear cubs for Galatea to play with. In Góngora it is more unusual still in its remoteness from the pastoral world and in its contrast with Acis's humble offering of fruit, butter and honey. It is, anachronistically, the work of a skilled oriental craftsman, a bow and carved ivory quiver from Malacca. With these as her attributes she will be, not Venus and Juno in one, but Venus and Cupid—beautiful and amorous:

> arco, digo, gentil, bruñida aljaba,
> obras ambas de artífice prolijo,
> y de Malaco rey a deidad Java
> alto don, según ya mi huésped dijo.
> De aguél la mano, de ésta el hombro agrava;
> convencida la madre, imita al hijo:
> serás a un tiempo en estos horizontes
> Venus del mar, Cupido de los montes. (457–64)
> [The handsome bow and burnished quiver were
> Works of laborious skill, which once had been
> Made for Malacca's king, a present rare,
> My guest asserted, for a Javan queen.
> That in your hand, this on your shoulder bear;
> Mother and son alike in you be seen;
> So may you, now the Venus of the sea,
> Also the Cupid of the mountains be.]

This unexpected gift adds to the pathetic irony of the song by establishing a connexion (and thus a second justification for the anachronism) with the imagery leading to Galatea's conquest by Acis. Unknown to Polyphemus, Cupid had already made her the quiver of one of his own arrows:

> Entre las ramas del que más se lava
> en el arroyo, mirto levantado,
> carcaj de cristal hizo, si no aljaba,
> su blanco pecho, de un arpón dorado. (241-4)
> [The loftiest myrtle boughs, whose lower part
> The stream most deeply washes, Cupid seeks;
> Her ivory bosom for his golden dart
> A crystal sheath, if not a quiver, makes.]

Bow and quiver are one example of the richer resources that Góngora can impart to his version of the giant's song. He gives it a wider meaning by greatly enlarging the framework of the fable into the dualism of life: white-black, beauty-ugliness, harmony-discord, love-death. Within this framework it is particularly moving that the grotesque giant should praise Galatea's beauty in the same imagery with which the poem had introduced her—whiter than the swan, as majestic as the peacock, with eyes more glittering than the stars:

> ¡Oh bella Galatea, más süave
> que los claveles que tronchó la aurora;
> blanca más que las plumas de aquel ave
> que dulce muere y en las aguas mora;
> igual en pompa al pájaro que, grave,
> su manto azul de tantos ojos dora
> cuantas el celestial zafiro estrellas!
> ¡Oh tú, que en dos incluyes las más bellas! (361-8)
> [Fair maiden, gentler than a flower bent low
> When dawn's first dewdrop on its petals lies,
> With plumage whiter than the swan can show,
> Who dwells upon the sea, and singing dies,
> Splendid as is the peacock, for although
> His azure mantle shines with golden eyes
> Thick as the stars that stud the sapphire zone,
> No two are lovelier, maiden, than your own.]

Remembering that Polyphemus has been identified with the destructive forces of nature and associated with death, we see in his yearning for the grace, whiteness and majesty of Galatea, in his worship of beauty, that the dualism of life is not a conflict of opposing principles. Violence and disorder do not just offset the harmony and creative power of nature; the real tragedy of life is that ugliness loves beauty. Beauty is the norm; it is the perfection to which all nature strives; it is the sole object of the love that pulsates in all creation. But nature falls short of her own standards; perfection is unattainable. Yet ugliness loves beauty; the imperfect yearns to possess the perfection that its own existence makes impossible. The 'inner woe' of Polyphemus (564–6) is the grief of nature at her own imperfection; it is the tears with which Galatea invokes the deities of the sea—

> Con lágrimas la ninfa solicita
> las deidades del mar   (493–4)

—and the *llanto pío* (503), the 'pitiful lamentation', with which her mother greets her son-in-law. The greatest imperfection of nature is death. This is ultimately the ugliness against which all her enduring beauty can never prevail.

Galatea is loved by both Acis and Polyphemus; through the one beauty attains to its creative fulfilment in love, through the other this love is extinguished. Death comes to Acis because of jealousy, which is the imperfection of love through frustration, as night is the imperfection of day and ugliness the imperfection that prevents beauty from reigning supreme. In accordance with the whole design of the poem, the murderous jealousy of Polyphemus is raised from the individual plane to that of the destructive imperfection of nature, on which he was placed at the beginning—the thunder and lightning of her storms:

> y al garzón viendo, cuantas mover pudo
> celoso trueno, antiguas hayas mueve:
> tal, antes que la opoca nube rompa,
> previene rayo fulminante trompa.

> Con vïolencia desgajó infinita,
> la mayor punta de la excelsa roca,
> que al joven, sobre quien la precipita,
> urna es mucha, pirámide no poca.   (485–92)

> [never storm displaced
> So many beech-trees as his jealous roar;

Thus thunder sounds its warning trumpet loud
Before the bolt bursts from a gloomy cloud.

The Cyclops, to prodigious effort stirred,
From the high cliff a massive fragment rent
Which, hurled below on Acis, soon conferred
An ample urn, and no light monument.]

The blood of Acis is turned to water and flows as a river into the
sea, welcomed by the nymph who is Galatea's mother. The con-
cluding line links closely the love and the death of Acis through
the correspondence of river and son-in-law, thus rounding of the
imagery that has associated love with death throughout the poem:
a Doris llega, que, con llanto pío,
yerno lo saludó, lo aclamó río. (503–4)
[And Doris, bathed in tears, to whom they run
Receives a river while she greets a son.]
It is justifiable to see in this conclusion, as R.O. Jones has done
(see above p. 55), 'distinctly a note of triumph', if one reads this
as Doris acclaiming a new divinity, the young man who rises out
of the sea as a river-god at the close of Ovid's narration: this is
Acis in a higher form of life. Doris can be prouder of a river than
of a human son-in-law. Góngora, however, neither mentions nor
describes the new river god, and the 'acclamation' is rather
muted by Doris's 'pitiful lamentation', which is the literal transla-
tion of *llanto pío*. To have to acclaim a river instead of greeting a
son-in-law can be, with this emphasis, the sorrow of existence.

This reading immediately brings to mind the traditional symbol-
ism of human life as a river running into the sea of death. Pellicer,
in his Góngora commentary of 1630 already referred to, states
that 'it is not inappropriate here to recall that old Castilian poem,
all the more worthy of esteem on that account, of Don Jorge
Manrique:
Nuestras vidas son los ríos
que van a dar en la mar,
que es el morir' etc.[99]
[Our lives are the rivers which finish up in the sea, which is
death.]
Pellicer also quotes the verse from *Ecclesiastes* (i, 7): 'All the
rivers run into the sea; yet the sea is not full; unto the place from

which the rivers come, thither they return again'. This passage had been traditionally interpreted by biblical commentators as an allegory of human mortality.[100] The following quatrain is from the sonnet *Salmo* XVIII by Quevedo, Góngora's contemporary:

Antes que sepa andar el pie, se mueve
camino de la muerte, donde envío
mi vida obscura: pobre y turbio río
que negro mar con altas ondas bebe.[101]

[Before man's foot learns to walk it is already moving towards death, whither I send my dark life: a poor and muddied river that the black sea drinks up with its high waves.]

Manrique's and Quevedo's poems are specifically on death, while Góngora's is a fable on love and jealousy; none-the-less there is nothing in *Polifemo* to prevent us from making these traditional associations. We are in a much better position today to go behind the rationalism, positivism and scientism of the nineteenth and early twentieth centuries and so understand the manner of thinking and feeling that was general until the eighteenth, whereby ideas about life were not confined to the surface appearances of objects and to the concepts logically derived from their differentiation. This was a type of mind that saw symbols, emblems and allegories below the level of realistic observation, and that discovered poetic truth through disparate correspondences. It is easier for us than it was for Pabst's generation to see beyond an aesthetic impressionism in *Polifemo*, for the associations of river with life and sea with death are consonant with the wide-ranging symbolism that modern anthropology has made us aware of.[102]

If, after reaching the river's acclamation by the sea, we look back on the poem, we see how important a place the sea assumes in the framework of the fable. It surrounds the island. Much emphasis is placed upon the sea-gods. With no justification in mythology Góngora makes the mermen Glaucus and Palaemon woo Galatea, who is herself a sea-nymph. Acis is the son of a sea-nymph. Polyphemus is the son of Neptune; and the presiding deity of the poem, Venus, was also born of the sea. In the light of Acis's metamorphosis it seems as if mankind, symbolically, is born of the sea and returns to the sea; as if life and death go hand in hand; as if, too, life were courted by death.

R. O. Jones holds that the sea in *Polifemo* 'does not symbolise . . . any ordinary conception of death since the sea, too, is abounding in life'. We are not speaking of 'any ordinary conception', but rather of the mythic 'Waters of Death' that underlie pagan, Judaic and Christian concepts. In any case, the realms of death were not, for classical paganism, uninhabited. Góngora was following his fable, but in adding to its framework in the way he did he must have had a *poetic* awareness of some sort of mythic symbolism, which need not have been conceptually or even consciously present in his mind.

The denial that the sea is a symbol of death enables Jones, in the passage quoted above (p. 55), to maintain that the poem is not 'pessimistic' but 'optimistic'. Why should it be either? To love life but to recognize its imperfections is not to be either an optimist or a pessimist—it is to accept reality as it is. Life and death are inseparable; so are love and jealousy, tenderness and violence, beauty and ugliness. The imperfections of nature do not make any less lovable the limited perfections she does attain, or any less beautiful the beauty she lavishes for us. No poet has felt more deeply or expressed with greater refinement the glory of life in the beauty and fertility of nature, the sensuous richness of material objects and the harmony of human love. But in praising beauty Góngora does not forget ugliness; in praising life he does not forget death or cease to feel the 'pitiful lamentation' it provokes. In consequence, Góngora's art has an assured poise and harmony.

The baroque style in *Polifemo*, highly mannered and elaborate though it is, has no strain or tension in it. It is not an arabesque, or overladen ornamentation in which details lose shape and purpose in a meaningless profusion of twists and turns. The organic conceits create groups of images that function as thematic symbols; as a result, the complex images run together with an ordered pattern in which no detail is out of place. The different threads of the pattern are never entangled or lost; with masterly control Góngora threads them in and out until the whole design is completed, until discordant correspondences or paradoxical contrasts are resolved in the final unity of the theme. Not only is this a unity that resolves the opposites with which the poem opens,

Either a vault that houses Vulcan's forge,

Or serves the bones of Typhon for a tomb (27–8),
and the one with which it closes,
    Receives a *river* while she greets a *son* (504);
it is also a unity that by a consistent and ordered development
links the end with the beginning—the forge/tomb with the son/
river, the volcano with the sea—in the oneness of love and death.
This controlled linking and fusion exist because of the assurance
in the unified experience that underlies the astonishing richness
of the imagery. This assurance is given to experience by the
creative intellectual imagination (*ingenio*), which manipulates
images in an ordered and functional way because it alone can
give order to the riot of the senses, control the clash of emotions
and harmonize the dichotomies of ideas. These characteristics of
Góngora's baroque art are due to the power of the conceit to
bring the disparate together by uniting in a universal correspond-
ence gods and men, land and sea, love and death, through a
series of separate correspondences between the animate and the
inanimate, men and creatures, the human and the material, etc.[103]
By stepping over ontological and logical categories, and the
structural divisions in the world of nature, the art of Wit was able
to harmonize feeling and thought. Góngora's poetry is highly
sensuous, but at the same time it could not be more intellectual.

   In form and structure *Polifemo* is one of the most accomplished
works of art in Spanish literature, rounded and finished. The
relation of form to content, of images to ideas, of narrative to
symbolism is perfect. It is full and elaborate in its details, yet the
poem as a whole gives the impression of astonishing conciseness;
it shows no squandering of a lavish artistry but is very tightly
packed. For all these reasons this is poetry of the very highest class.

   In conclusion, a few words should be said on the poem's alleged
Neoplatonism.[104] To see it as possibly influenced by Plotinus's
view of the universe (see above p. 55), seems an attempt to
bridge an unbridgeable gulf. There is a 'philosophy of life' in a
poetic sense in *Polifemo*, but it is essentially a pastoral, erotic and
(above all) witty and 'ingenious' fable, which, as such, can have
no connexion with the lofty spiritual idealism of Plotinus's cosmic
mysticism. None-the-less, the poem may be considered to derive
from a platonic tradition, as was suggested earlier in this Introduc-
tion. It is in the line of a poetic theory that has been called

'platonic'; it is connected with a 'philosophy of correspondences' that has affinities with fifteenth-century platonism and with the sixteenth-century Neoplatonism of the philosophers of Nature. This connexion is one of cultural climate; it makes only for a loose platonism, and one that is not doctrinal. There is a very fine meditative Spanish poem of the sixteenth century whose doctrinal Neoplatonism is evident. This is the *Carta para Arias Montano sobre la contemplación de Dios y los requisitos de ella* [Letter to Arias Montano on the Contemplation of God and its Requisites], by Francisco Aldana.[105] Here the contemplation of the beauty of Nature (marvellously communicated in the wonder at the variety and intricate artistry of sea-shells) leads to the contemplation of Creation and on to the apprehension of the Creator and to the yearning for mystical union with him. To look for the influence of Plotinus in this *Epistle* would not be far-fetched, though it would not be necessary. Góngora's *Polifemo*, on the other hand, is close to the very different world of Ovid.

7. *Verse Structure*

To the conclusion that *Polifemo* is poetry of the very highest class there still has to be added the evidence of its architectural and musical craftsmanship. No reader can fail to become aware of the parallelistic construction of its verses. The eight-line stanza is in nearly every case divided into halves by a heavy stop, and reveals a symmetrical structure in other ways also. Lines can be conceptually and syntactically paired:

> bóveda de las fraguas de Vulcano,
>
> o tumba de los huesos de Tifeo (27–8)

There is a double pairing in

> la serba, a quien le da rugas el heno;
> la pera, de quien fue cuna dorada
> la rubia paja, y—pálida tutora—
> la niega avara, y pródiga la dora. (77–80)

Here the lines are paired by a repetition of the syntax: the first pair by noun-relative-verb-subject, the second pair by the balance of the words helped by the linking vowel assonance of —*a paja* / *avara* and the near assonance of the proparoxytones *pálida* and *pródiga*, these linking words being in the same metrical position in their respective lines. Further, the third line has the syntactical symmetry adjective-noun/adjective-noun, and the fourth the chiastic symmetry of object+verb—adjective/conjunction/adjective—object+verb, with the further parallelism of the semantic contrast between the two adjectives ('miserly' and 'prodigal'). The halving of individual lines, as in these last two examples, either by repetition or by chiasmus, is the most frequent single structural feature, especially common as a resounding last line of the stanzas. Many examples were noticed in the course of the above analysis of conceits and theme. Here are others: 'peinar el viento, fatigar la selva' (8); 'en carro de cristal, campos de plata' (120); 'rinden las vacas y fomentan el robre' (200); 'grillos de nieve fue, plumas de hielo' (224).

The various ways in which Góngora reveals his predilection for a two-part symmetry has been studied by Dámaso Alonso with his usual mastery.[106] This often meticulous symmetry is rare, to this degree, in other poets; it is so far removed from the practice of modern poets that it must strike the reader who comes to it for the first time as a perhaps tiresome mannerism. We have seen that it has an essential function to play in the conceptual structure of the poem, and therefore in the conception of the theme. Although this is not so in every instance it is impossible to separate this element from the rest of the poem; this constriction of verbal and syntactical patterns is part of the over-all unity of the poem, giving it its statuesque, almost hieratic, quality.

What makes these mannered patterns readily accepted—indeed, what allows them to pass unnoticed by all but the most attentive readers—is the music of Góngora's lines. He is one of the most melodious of all Spanish poets and his music has a subtlety not found later in Romantic and Modernist verse, where novel musical effects are generally the result of unusual metres. Góngora extracts the maximum musicality from the Italian hendecasyllabic line, and very expressive sound effects from forms of alliteration, as in the often-quoted line 'infame *tur*ba de noc*tur*nas aves' (39). Dámaso Alonso's method of stylistic analysis has revealed the full extent of Góngora's craftsmanship in these respects. But further reasons for the exceptional musicality of *Polifemo* have been disclosed by Colin Smith, who detected the fact that Góngora arranges vowel sounds in symmetrical patterns (and, one may add, the astonishing fact that these are the same symmetrical patterns in which he arranges parts of speech). What follows is a summary of Smith's paper *La musicalidad del 'Polifemo'*.[107] These patterns are possible in Spanish by the phonetic simplicity of its vowel system (a feature, also, of Italian). In the line just quoted the threefold repetition of the group of letters *a-e* (inf*a*m*e*, turb*a* d*e*, *a*v*e*s) is the repetition of the same two sounds.

The commonest example of 'vowel music' in *Polifemo* is the echo-like repetition at the end of a line of the same two vowels in the two syllables of its beginning:

d*e* m*á*s ecos que unió cáñamo y c*e*r*a*   (91)
a l*a* de viento, cuando no sea c*a*m*a*   (215)
p*i*s*a*ndo la dudosa luz del d*í*a   (72)

Such repetition constitutes a frequent vowel pattern in the poem. Though it must have become a habit of composition it is not likely to have been unconscious in every case; in the second example the highly distorted syntax (see the note to this line) seems to have no other function than to produce the phonic balance of the beginning and the end.

There can be repetition of three or four vowel sounds in the same position:

s*er* d*e* l*a* negra noche nos lo *e*ns*e*ñ*a*   (38)
l*a* c*a*v*e*rn*a* profunda que *a* l*a* peñ*a*   (36)

There is a five-vowel pattern in the following astonishing line, where perfect symmetry is achieved by the vowel repetition between the two long groups:

en pie, sombra capaz es mi persona   (411)
e i-e o-a / a-a / e i e-o-a

This is not meaningless virtuosity. Each of these lines, especially the last, is given a special melodiousness by the phonic repetition. This repetition can be in inverse order (i.e. chiastic):

c*on* *el* pincel que le clavó su p*ech*o   (272)
G*a*l*a*t*e*a lo diga, s*a*lt*e**a*d*a*   (304)

All this is what Smith calls Góngora's 'normal' sound patterns. They become more complex when there is a threefold repetition (not necessarily symmetrically placed):

Con lágrimas la ninfa solicita   (493)
- - / i-a / - / i-a / - - / i-a

Or two pairs of chiastic assonances:

Su horrenda voz, no su dolor interno   (465)
- / o-é / - / ó-o / - o-ó / - / é-o

where it will be noticed that the four groups are symmetrically placed syllabically.

The name Galatea, itself so euphonious, invariably enriches musically the lines that accompany it. In the following example the rhyme *ea*, extended to *latea*, produces a marvellous assonance of *a* and *e*:

Galatea.

Pisa la arena, que en la arena adoro
cuantas el blanco pie conchas platea   (372-4)
     a-a-e-a
- / a-a-a-e-a / e-e / a-a-e-a-a / - -
a-a-e-a / [co] - ié - [co] / a-a-e-a.

The phonic symmetry of this last line is unbelievably skilful; as a result its melody is exquisite. The most elaborate musical effects are produced when three or four assonance groups, of from two to five vowels, are interwoven within one stanza. An example is the second (lines 9–16), at which the reader may wish to try his hand on his own.

The last lines quoted show an example of 'rich rhyme'—the two obligatory rhyming syllables, -*ea*, extended to three, -*latea*. It should be noted, however, that the rhyme is in fact even richer since these three rhyming syllables are in each case preceded by the vowel *a*: -*alatea*, -*as platea*. This enrichment of rhyme by assonance as well as by additional consonants in *Polifemo* has been studied in a second paper by Colin Smith.[108] The enrichment is frequent in the end rhymes:

tal, antes que la opaca nub*e r*ompa,
previene rayo fulminant*e t*rompa.   (487-8)

But it is also found in the other rhymes:

El ronco arrullo al jove*n soli*cita;	A
mas, con desvíos Galat*ea s*uaves,	B
a su audacia los térmi*nos lim*ita,	A
y el aplauso al concento d*e las* aves.	B
Entre las ondas y la fruta, *im*ita	A
Acis al siempre ayuno en p*enas* graves (321-6)	B

Colin Smith sums up this aspect of his *Polifemo* studies as follows:
The *Polifemo* must be unique, . . . in world literature, for its

purely musical qualities, to which the supplementary echoes of rich rhyme contribute greatly. As one studies the various types of word-music in the poem, one begins to see even greater reason for the liberties the poet took with word-order. The logical exposition of 'sense' of the intellectual kind was of very little interest to Góngora. His sense is of the sensory and sensual kind, and much of it is conveyed by word-music.

To explore and analyse Góngora's artistry in one particular aspect [rich rhyme]—even in what seems at first sight to be a very unexciting aspect—is to realize anew what an astonishing creation the *Polifemo* is. Here are no casual conjunctions of sounds, but a construction of such artifice that the process of its building seems to the ordinary mortal the more mysterious the more it is investigated, the more divinely inspired.[109]

This fine statement would be unexceptionable but for the last two sentences of the penultimate paragraph. It is true that Góngora in this poem was not specially interested in 'the *logical* exposition of "sense" of the intellectual kind', but the *witty* formulation and exposition of intellectual sense was a prime concern with him. This kind of sense combines with the sensory and the sensual to produce what it is surely justifiable to call a *total* work of poetic art, one in which none of these three elements is weakened by its communication through either of the other two. Most readers may continue in the future, as has been the case in the past, to attach little importance (some even none at all) to the poem's *agudeza* and to the ideas it packs so tightly into the poetic form, but to ignore the fact that Góngora consciously strove to create an art of the mind—*arte de ingenio*—is to simplify his artistry. This, in effect, is to lessen his achievement, even if we were to hold (as I do not) that this simplification is an aesthetic improvement.

8. '*Culteranismo*'

Góngora's fame (or notoriety) as a Latinizer of the Spanish language has obscured the fame as an *ingenio* that his contemporaries acknowledged. His *culteranismo* has been studied by Dámaso Alonso, especially in *La lengua poética de Góngora* (1935), and by Antonio Vilanova in *Las fuentes y los temas del Polifemo de*

Góngora (1957). A few examples will here be given to illustrate this aspect of his style.

Every language increases its vocabulary by borrowing from others. Romance languages naturally borrow most extensively from their parent, Latin. Such borrowings were continuous from the fifteenth century to the seventeenth. Góngora is the last of the major Spanish poets whose style abounds in Latinisms. Juan de Mena (1411–56) was the first. The abundance of neologisms in *Polifemo* and *Soledades* struck contemporaries as pedantry. The anti-*culteranos*, with Quevedo at their head, listed the objectionable words that ought to be banished from use. What surprises us today is that the vast majority of such words are now normal and indispensable currency. *Caliginoso* (37) still has a literary ring, but *nocturno* (172) is now colloquial. The most extraordinary instance is *joven*. One would not think that Spanish could ever have been a working language without it; yet, though introduced in the thirteenth century, it did not become established till after Góngora's time. Its occurrence in *Polifemo* (lines 121, 321, 491) was, for contemporary readers, yet another example of affectation.

'Learned' words in *Polifemo* that became, sooner or later, part of the everyday lexicon of Spanish include, for example, these: *formidable* (41), *melancólico* (42), *esplendor* (111), *venerar* (198), *fomentar* (200), *inmóvil* (262), *disposición* (274), *admirar* (275, 276), *cóncavo* (309), *limitar* (323), *prodigioso* (348), *derivar* (390), *inquieto* (396), *delicia* (445), *interno* (465). All these Latinisms, and the great majority of all the others, had already been used in poetry before Góngora. If he helped to naturalize such words, as he must have done, he deserves posterity's praise. Góngora's predecessor, Fernando de Herrera, who also preferred learned to common words, earned not the censure of his contemporaries, but the title of 'the divine'. Probably no-one would have taken exception to Góngora's occasional use of such words; what must have irritated his contemporaries was their practically exclusive use. There is no stanza of *Polifemo* that has not at least one, and generally several, Latinisms. For example:

Con *vïolencia* desgajó infinita,
la mayor punta de la *excelsa* roca,
que al *joven*, sobre quien la *precipita*,
urna es mucha, *pirámide* no poca.

Con lágrimas la *ninfa solicita*
las *deidades* del mar, que Acis *invoca*:
concurren todas, y el peñasco duro
la sangre que *exprimió*, cristal fue puro.   (489–96)

Examples of learned borrowings that were still rare are *torrente* (61), *cerúleo* (121), *intonso* (282), *neutro* ('impartial', 423), *opaco* (487). The following are words or usages that have not become established. *Culto* (228) is used in the sense of 'worshipped', 'venerated' (past participle of *colo*). *Vago* (467) is used in its primary Latin sense of 'wandering'. *Vulto* (285) for 'face' is a pure Latinism; earlier (257) Góngora had used it with its normal Spanish meaning of 'figure', 'form' (and different spelling, *bulto*). *Librar* (258) is not *librar<liberare*, but the Latin *librare* ('to balance'), a neologism apparently due to Góngora alone. The use of *impedir* in the sense of 'to block, fill up' (386) is also confined to him. Other neologisms coined by him, or of which only one or two examples have been found elsewhere, are *tutor(a)* (79), *vincular* (208), *conculcar* (469), and *dirimir* (479).

This Latinization of vocabulary had represented, from the time of Juan de Mena, the constant endeavour to ennoble the language of poetry by avoiding words that had become or were becoming hackneyed, and thus to keep the 'high' literary style at a constantly elevated level, maintaining the dignity of the highest type of poetry by keeping its diction above that of everyday speech. The same motive impelled Góngora to greater daring than any predecessor or contemporary in Latinizing his syntax. The following line 'vagas el pie, sacrílegas el cuerno' (467) exemplifies the so-called Greek Accusative; the adjectives agree, not with the nouns they accompany, but with the subject of the sentence, *cabras*; the goats' feet and horns are 'in the accusative case' (wandering as regards their feet, and sacrilegious as regards their horns). Góngora's frequent placing of a relative clause between the article or demonstrative qualifying the antecedent noun and the noun itself is a classical construction. 'Estas que me dictó rimas sonoras' (1): (Literally: 'These, which have been dictated to me, sonorous verses'), Or:

este (que, de Neptuno hijo fiero,
de un ojo ilustra el orbe de su frente,
émulo casi del mayor lucero)

cíclope ...

Este is the demonstrative and *cíclope* the noun it qualifies; they are separated by a long relative clause.

An example of the separation of article and noun is

Entre las ramas del que más se lava

en el arroyo, mirto levantado (241-2)

where the article is in *del* and its noun is *mirto*.

This displacement of normal word order is the Gongorine hyperbaton. An adjective is frequently separated from its noun in ways that correct syntax does not permit. He writes *nocturno el lobo* (172) and *gallardo el joven* (298) instead of *el lobo nocturno* and *el gallardo joven*. Hyperbata of course also give to the poet's Spanish a Latin ring and flavour; but it will be found that in nearly every case the purpose is not artificial (as mere Latinization would imply), for the displacement of word-order gives a special expressiveness to the phrase or sentence. It must be realized that Spanish is exceptional among the Romance languages by reason of the fluidity of its word-order. A displaced word becomes more emphatic in its unusual position; this is especially the case if a word that normally comes at the beginning of a sentence or clause is placed at the end, and *vice versa*. For instance: 'que dijera que no, es natural, pero el insulto no me lo explico' ('That he should have said no is natural, but I cannot understand *the insult*': to get the equivalent emphasis in English one has to change the construction, 'but what I can't understand is the insult'). Or: 'Comida te puedo dar pero no dinero' ('I can give you *food*, but not money'). Expressiveness through emphasis is what Góngora obtains by hyperbaton, whether the phrase or clause in question be long or short. Thus if the first line read *Estas rimas sonoras que me dictó* ..., we would pay no particular attention to a conventional phrase. But by being brought to the emphatic line-end and given what will be the first rhyme, *rimas sonoras* strikes us with an expressive force. Góngora could have put these two words at the end of a line of normal word-order, but he would not thereby have ensured the same effect, for the sentence would have been 'ordinary' and the expressiveness depends upon our being struck by its 'extraordinariness'.

The displacement of adjectives produces beautiful effects of this kind. The hyperbaton in these cases does not shock as it would in other languages because, in Spanish, adjectives can so often be used as adverbs. 'Nocturno el lobo de las sombras nace' (172) gives a special expressive force to 'the *night-prowling* wolf', which in English can only be conveyed by the tone of the voice. But in any case the hyperbaton is not as strange in Spanish as a similar word-order would be in English, because it is syntactically equivalent to 'nocturnally, the wolf is born from the shadows'. A marvellous effect is attained by the displacement of an adjective to the end of the line in

cuando al clavel el joven atrevido
las dos hojas le chupa carmesíes, (331–2)

It is necessary to pause for a second or two before *carmesíes* and then speak it with a slightly stronger emphasis than the rhyme would ordinarily give it. Emphasis is also given to the important accompanying word *clavel* by its displacement from its normal position after the verb. The normal word-order would be in Spanish what it is in English, but we must in English italicize the words to which Góngora's order gives a natural emphasis: 'when the daring young man sucks the two *crimson* petals of the *carnation*'. That this kind of expressiveness, produced by hyperbaton, can add to the musical quality of the poetry was noted by Colin Smith in the case of the line 'a la de viento, cuando no sea cama' (215). The same justification can also be given to the exquisitely musical line analysed above 'cuantas el blanco pie conchas platea' (374), where the displacement of *cuantas* away from its noun *conchas* produces the amazing and melodious assonantal symmetry, a-a-e-a / co-ie-co / a-a-e-a. All this is poetry moulding syntax to aesthetic ends, but doing it in accordance with, and not against, the genius of the language. The objections that have been raised to the Miltonic style do not apply to Góngora, who added to the vocabulary of Spanish, and took liberties with its syntax, by developing its natural potentialities. This is still further evidence of his consummate mastery of the language of poetry.

Notes to the Introduction

1 The best survey is René Wellek, 'The Concept of Baroque in Literary Scholarship', with a 'Postscript 1962', in *Concepts of Criticism* (New Haven and London 1963) 69–127.

2 This classification was suggested for French and English literatures by Odette de Mourgues, *Metaphysical, Baroque and Précieux Poetry* (Oxford 1953).

3 Frank J. Warnke, *European Metaphysical Poetry* (New Haven and London 1961) 3. In a more recent work the same author admits Mannerism (which he, surely rightly, rejects as a term for a period) as an alternative for Metaphysical. 'The variety of literary phenomena during the Baroque age is, I have proposed, the source of the arguments over terminology that so often obscure its study. At least two trends, or, as I have called them, options, are recurrently perceptible amid this variety—the spare, witty, intellectual, paradoxical trend typified by Donne, Herbert, Marvell, Sponde, Quevedo, Huygens, and Fleming; and the ornate, exclamatory, emotional and extravagant trend typified by Crashaw, Gryphius, Marino, d'Aubigné, Góngora, and Vondel. The latter option—for many authorities the quintessential Baroque—might for convenience's sake be designated as "High Baroque". The former option—the style of "Metaphysical" poetry—might be designated as "Mannerist". The latter term would, so used, have the advantage of including not only the Metaphysical poets but also such figures as Webster, Gracián, Sir Thomas Browne, Pascal, and the early Corneille.' But he adds: 'The Baroque age simply will not lend itself to any simpler schematization as far as its style, or styles, are concerned.' (*Versions of Baroque: European Literature in the Seventeenth Century* [New Haven and London 1972] 11–12.) While a more general term than Metaphysical is certainly required, the appropriateness of Mannerism for this purpose seems very doubtful since intellectual agility is not one of its connotations.

4 James Smith, 'On Metaphysical Poetry', in *Scrutiny* (1933), many

times reprinted, the latest being in his posthumous *Shakespearian and Other Essay* (Cambridge 1974) 262–78.

5 op. cit., 276.

6 For an account of these terms see Andrée Collard, *Nueva poesía: conceptismo, culteranismo en la crítica española* (2nd ed., Madrid 1971). This useful book is marred by the belief that anti-Gongorism had an anti-semitic motivation, Góngora being of Jewish descent. For this there is no evidence whatever beyond the insults that were irresponsibly bandied about in personal polemics.

7 Republished in Antonio Gallego Morell, *Garcilaso de la Vega y sus comentaristas* (Granada 1966) 281–580.

8 See Antonio Vilanova, 'Preceptistas españoles de los siglos XVI y XVII', in *Historia General de las literaturas hispánicas*, ed. Guillermo Díaz-Plaja, III (Madrid 1953) 567–692.

9 Edited by A. Porqueras Mayo in the *Biblioteca de Antiguos Libros Hispánicos*, Serie A, vols. 25–6 (Madrid 1958).

10 There is a modern edition in the *Biblioteca de Antiguos Libros Hispánicos*, Serie A, 6 (Madrid 1946).

11 Vilanova (op. cit. 643) was the first to see this identity of aim in the two movements. For a study of the different kinds of difficulty sought by *culteranos* and *conceptistas* see Fernando Lázaro Carreter, 'Sobre la dificultad conceptista', in *Estudios dedicados a Menéndez Pídal*, VI (Madrid 1956) 355–86.

12 The Latin text has been published with a Polish translation in Maciej Kazimierz Sarbiewski, *Wyklady Poetyki* (*Praecepta Poetica*), ed. Stanislaw Skimina, Biblioteka Pizarzów Polskich, Seria B, Nr. 5 (Braslaw-Krakow 1958).

13 Because of the practical impossibility of separating Góngora's *conceptismo* from his *culteranismo* Dámaso Alonso has divided the Spanish literary Baroque into 'Gongorism, an ornamental and sensuous elaboration, intermingled with *conceptista* complexity', and 'Pure *conceptismo*, a conceptual complexity obtained in part by processes not unlike those of Gongorism, but without the sensuous and ornamental elaboration' (*Góngora y el 'Polifemo'*, 5th ed. [Madrid 1967] I, 89). There is danger, perhaps, in the term 'pure *conceptismo*', as there is in 'pure Wit'. Since in Alonso's definitions Wit appears in both styles, its status as the basic, common Baroque style is confirmed.

14 Single poems by Góngora appeared during his lifetime in printed anthologies, but he himself never sent to the press any selection of his output. It was rare for Spanish poets in the sixteenth and seventeenth centuries to publish their own works. Lope de Vega was a notable exception, but he was a professional writer earning

his living by literature. 'The non-professional author wanted to maintain the amateur pose. Though gentlemen might write poems, no gentleman would have them printed, because others would suspect that he was greedy for money or praise' (Edward M. Wilson, *Some Aspects of Spanish Literary History* [The Taylorian Lecture, Oxford 1967] 10).

15 The standard biography is by Miguel Artigas, *Don Luis de Góngora y Argote: Biografía y estudio crítico* (Madrid 1925). Much new material has come to light since its publication: for the bibliography see Dámaso Alonso, op. cit., I, 270-1; this work also contains the best short life, I, 35-58.

16 Francisco Cascales, a leading theorist of the time, summed up the case against *Polifemo* as follows: 'it is quite clear that the obscurity of the *Polifemo* is inexcusable; for it does not arise from any recondite doctrine but from the ambiguity of the frequently used hyperbaton and from the metaphors which are so continuous that one constantly discloses another, and which at times are even placed on top of each other' ('bien claro consta que la obscuridad del *Polifemo* no tiene excusa; pues no nace de recóndita doctrina, sino del ambagioso hipérbato tan frecuente y de las metáforas tan continuas que se descubren unas a otras, y aun a veces están unas sobre otras'); *Cartas filológicas* [published 1634 but written before 1626], ed. Justo García Soriano (Clásicos Castellanos, Madrid 1930) I, 194-5.

17 *Cancionero de 1628*, ed. José M. Blecua (Madrid 1945) 467-73.

18 *Epistolario*, Nr. 127; in *Obras completas de don Luis de Góngora y Argote*, ed. Juan and Isabel Millé y Giménez (Madrid n.d.) 1148-50. Góngora's reply is Epistolario, Nr. 2, 954-8. There is another undated edition of this work with different pagination.

19 'Eso mismo hallará V. m. en mis "Soledades", si tiene capacidad para quitar la corteza y descubrir lo misterioso que encubren' (ibid., 796). R. O. Jones took 'misterioso' to mean a hidden 'philosophy' within the poem [see following note] which he interpreted as the traditional praise of Nature and of the pastoral life developed into anti-commercialism. But *misterio* is one of the commonest terms in Gracián's *Agudeza* (as also in Calderón's *autos sacramentales*), where it denotes a statement or juxtaposition of ideas so enigmatic at first sight that the reader senses a significance that he feels compelled to unravel. What Góngora is saying is that a superficial reading of the *Soledades* finds them incomprehensible; a more careful reading detects the existence of a significance that is worth penetrating.

20 I quote the original before discussing R. O. Jones's interpretation:

'Demás que honra me ha causado hacerme escuro a los ignorantes, que esa [es] la distinción de los hombres doctos, hablar de manera que a ellos les parezca griego; pues no se han de dar las piedras preciosas a animales de cerda . . . pues si deleitar el entendimiento es darle razones que le concluyan y se midan con su contento, descubierto lo que está debajo de esos tropos, por fuerza el entendimiento ha de quedar convencido y convencido, satisfecho: demás que como el fin de el entendimiento es hacer presa en verdades, que por eso no le satisface nada si no es la primera verdad, conforme a aquella sentencia de San Agustín: *Inquietum est cor nostrum, donec requiescat in te*, en tanto quedará más deleitado, cuanto, obligándole a la especulación por la obscuridad de la obra, fuera hallando debajo de las sombras de la obscuridad asimilaciones a su concepto' (ibid. 956–7). R. O. Jones interpreted this passage as follows: 'Góngora's justification of his obscurity is itself somewhat obscure but I take "lo misterioso" [see preceding note] to be some general theme lying behind the profusion of incident and image in the poem. Through his quotation from St. Augustine (from *Confessions*, 1) Góngora more than hints that that theme is for him the ultimate truth of all. "Asimilaciones a su concepto" are (I see no alternative reading) to be interpreted as "asimilaciones [resemblances or approximations] al concepto de la primera verdad". Góngora seems to be claiming that the mind, puzzling over the multitudinous images, allusions and tropes of the *Soledades*, is led to an understanding of the source of all truth; which, in terms of seventeenth-century orthodoxy, one might suppose to be God. And yet God is nowhere mentioned in the poem; and even here, in the letter, Góngora seems to be studiously avoiding a name in favour of a philosophical abstraction. Too little effort has been devoted to the "especulación" that Góngora wished to provoke' ('Neoplatonism and the *Soledades*', in *Bulletin of Hispanic Studies*, XL [1963] 1–2). The 'First Truth' could not mean anything else but God; the admitted irrelevance of this to the context of letter and poem makes this interpretation far-fetched. Punctuating part of the long period as a parenthesis, as I do in my translation, makes it easier to see its natural construction.

21 For an account of the polemics and controversies see Miguel Artigas, op. cit., cap. XIV and Appendixes IV–VII; also Dámaso Alonso, op. cit., cap. III.

22 They had been published in 1627, the year of his death, but this edition was withdrawn after charges were made that it contained improper poems that Góngora himself had not wanted published.

23 'Función estructural de las pluralidades: (En la octava real)', in *Estudios y ensayos gongorinos* (Madrid 1955) 200–21.

24 Eugenio Donato, 'Tesauro's Poetics: Through the Looking Glass', in *MLN*, LXXVIII (1963) 15, 17.

25 This claim and the conclusions Donato draws are perhaps questionable. It would be a mistake to conclude that what he says of Tesauro's attitude to Marino applies also to Gracián and Góngora. Gracián did indeed find an imperfection in Góngora: a lack of 'moral teaching' and of a weighty subject-matter (*gravedad*) to match the 'heroic' style (*El criticón*, Crisi IV). By this he meant that there was a nobler sphere to human life than the pastoral and a nobler experience than the erotic. He did not accuse Góngora of departing from morality or reality.

26 'De suerte que se puede definir el concepto: Es un acto del entendimiento, que exprime la correspondencia que se halla entre los objetos. La misma consonancia o correlación artificiosa exprimida, es la sutileza objetiva ... Esta correspondencia es genérica a todos los conceptos, y abraza todo el artificio del ingenio, que aunque éste sea por contraposición y disonancia, aquello mismo es artificiosa conexión de los objectos' (*Agudeza y arte de ingenio*, Disc. II, [ed. E. Correa Calderón, Clásicos, Castalia, Madrid 1969, I 55–6]).

27 These are the lines as quoted by Gracián. The accepted reading of the second line is 'porque más cerca muriese' (*Obras completas*, ed. Millé, 32).

28 *Agudeza*, Disc. xlviii; ed. cit., II, 149.

29 Antonio Vilanova, *Las fuentes y los temas del 'Polifemo' de Góngora* (Madrid 1957).

30 'Mas el nervio del estilo consiste en la intensa profundidad del verbo ... Preñado ha de ser el verbo, no hinchado; que signifique, no que resuene; verbos con fondo, donde se engolfe la atención, donde tenga en qué cebarse la comprensión' (*Agudeza*, Disc. LX, ed. cit., II, 234).

31 *Agudeza*, Disc. xix; ed. cit., I, 198–9.

32 Bodo Müller, *Gongoras Metaphorik: Versuch einer Typologie* (Wiesbaden 1963) 164–5, 25–8.

33 Op. cit., 219–20. Müller's limited approach is valuable in other respects. On the level of structural types it shows in considerable detail Góngora's connexion with tradition—the classical rhetoricians, the Italian poets and the Renaissance theorists.

34 *Góngora y el Polífemo*, ed. cit., I, 90.

35 'The writers of tractates on the conceit began, like their predecessors of the *cinquecento*, by dividing the "form" of a literary creation

from its content. They stated the problem in the same way and agreed that the content was either moral or immoral and consisted of things, actions or thoughts. The "form", however, was for our theorists the true key to the work of art. It was imparted by the activity of "ingegno" or "wit", and created that element of the work of literary art which is esthetically pleasing. This conception reversed the emphasis of the *cinquecento* critics. It was as a reaction to their predecessors that the "concettisti" turned most of their attention to the study and analysis of the "form".

'It was this same emphasis on form that led Cardinal Sforza-Pallavicino [1646] to observe that the originality of an author is always to be determined by the "form", since the content *qua* content is never original.' (J. A. Mazzeo, 'A Seventeenth-Century Theory of Metaphysical Poetry', in *Romanic Review*, XLII [1951] 246. Reprinted in his volume *Renaissance and Seventeenth-Century Studies* [New York and London 1964] 31.)

36 Terence Hawkes, *Metaphor* (*The Critical Idiom*, no. 25; London 1972) 55. See also 9–11, and for a more modern way of expressing this (in terms of interaction between vehicle and tenor) 60–3.

37 Terence Hawkes, op. cit., 18, 20, 21. The reference is to Rosemond Tuve, *Elizabethan and Metaphysical Imagery* (Chicago 1947), perhaps to the last chapter, which is a most valuable account of the sixteenth and seventeenth centuries' conception of poetry, contrasted with the modern standpoints hostile to them.

38 K. K. Ruthven, *The Conceit* (*The Critical Idiom*, no. 4; London 1969) 9–11. The reference to T. E. May is to 'Gracián's Idea of the *Concepto*', in *Hispanic Review*, XVIII (1950) 27–9.

39 J. A. Mazzeo, 'Metaphysical Poetry and the Poetic of Correspondence', in *Journal of the History of Ideas*, XIV (1953) 222, 223, 230, 232–3. Reprinted in his *Renaissance and Seventeenth-Century Studies* (New York and London 1964) 45, 47, 54, 58.

40 This assertion, and the support that follows, are tentative only. If there is indeed a philosophy on which the Poetic of Correspondence is based, it should probably be looked for in this context, but this is a connexion that, if I am not mistaken, still remains to be investigated.

41 Frederick Copleston, *A History of Philosophy*, vol. III (London 1953) 233. I am indebted to this invaluable work for what follows.

42 Copleston, op. cit., III, 240.

43 See the section on 'Coincidence of Contraries' in Dorothea Waley Singer, *Giordano Bruno: his Life and Thought* (New York 1950) 80–6.

44 E. Sarmiento, 'Gracián's "Agudeza y arte de ingenio"', in *Modern*

Language Review, XXVII (1932) 280–92, 420–9. This is the most lucid exposition. More complex and subtle are the two studies by T. E. May, 'An Interpretation of Gracián's *Agudeza y arte de ingenio*', in *Hispanic Review*, XVI (1948) 275–300; and 'Gracián's Idea of the *Concepto*', ibid., XVIII (1950) 15–41. Mazzeo's 'A Seventeenth-century Theory of Metaphysical Poetry', loc. cit., barely touches on Gracián. The fine study by S. L. Bethell, 'Gracián, Tesauro, and the Nature of Metaphysical Wit' (*The Northern Miscellany of Literary Criticism*, no. 1 [1953] 19–40) is much better on Tesauro than on Gracián. Virginia R. Foster's *Baltasar Gracián* (Twayne World Authors Series, Boston 1975) is very disappointing. Two chapters are devoted to *Agudeza* ('The Aesthetics of Conceit' and 'The Concept of Poetry'), both of which give exceedingly brief summaries of Gracián's expository statements with no clarifying commentary. Most of the writers and poets whom Gracián admired and quoted from are named, but none of the examples of their Wit that Gracián selected and commented on are reproduced. Telescoped definitions without examples and analyses of conceits are singularly unhelpful. However, the latest book on Gracián is one of the best, certainly in English: Theodore L. Kassier, *The Truth Disguised: Allegorical Structure and Technique in Gracián's 'Criticón'* (Tamesis Books, London 1976). This deals indirectly with the *Agudeza*, in that it analyses Gracián's long allegorical 'novel' in relation to his theory of Wit. The reader will find this theory expounded and exemplified more fully and in a wider context than I have attempted above.

45 Baltasar Gracián, *Agudeza y arte de ingenio*, ed. Evaristo Correa Calderón (Clásicos Castalia, Madrid 1969), *Al Letor*, I, 45. All references will be to this edition, with the number of the *Discurso* as well as volume and page.

46 'Si el percibir la agudeza acredita de águila, el producirla empeñará en ángel; empleo de querubines, y elevación de hombres, que nos remonta a extravagante jerarquía' (Disc. ii; I, 51).

47 By 'artistry', here and in what follows, I am translating *artificio*, which in Gracián's usage is not our modern 'artifice'. The adjective *artificioso*, (which is not synonymous with *artificial*) is particularly difficult to render in English: it means artistic, skilful, subtle, creative, inventive.

48 'Consiste, pues, este artificio conceptuoso, en una primorosa concordancia, en una armónica correlación entre dos o tres cognoscibles extremos, expresada por un acto del entendimiento . . . De suerte que se puede definir el concepto: Es un acto del entendimiento, que exprime la correspondencia que se halla entre los

objectos. La misma consonancia o correlación artificiosa expri-
mida, es la sutileza objectiva ... Esta correspondencia es genérica
a todos los conceptos, y abraza todo el artificio del ingenio, que
aunque éste sea tal vez por contraposición y disonancia, aquello
mismo es artificiosa conexión de los objectos' (Disc. ii; 1, 55–6).
The paragraph before this quotation summarized pp. 51–4 of this
Discourse.

49 'La primera distinción sea entre la agudeza de perspicacia y la de
artificio; y ésta es el asunto de nuestra Arte. Aqúella tiende a dar
alcance a las dificultosas verdades, descubriendo la más recóndita.
Ésta, no cuidando tanto deso, afecta la hermosura sutil; aquélla es
más útil, ésta deleitable; aquélla es todas las Artes y Ciencias, en
sus actos y sus hábitos; ésta por recóndita y extraordinaria, no
tenía casa fija' (*Agudeza*, Disc. iii; 1, 58). 'Let the first distinction be
between the Wit of perspicacity and that of artifice; the latter is
the subject of our Art. The former tends to track down difficult
truths, discovering the most hidden. The latter, being less con-
cerned with that, aims at subtle beauty; the former is more useful,
the latter pleasing; the former comprises all the Arts and Sciences,
in their acts and their habits; the latter, because it is recondite and
out of the ordinary has had no fixed home'.

50 For the meaning of adjuncts see the quotation on pp. 40–1.

51 'La agudeza compuesta consta de muchos actos y partes princi-
pales, si bien se unen en la moral y artificiosa trabazón de un
discurso ... composición artificiosa del ingenio, en que se erige
máquina sublime, no de columnas ni arquitrabes, sino de asuntos y
de conceptos' (*Agudeza*, Disc. iii; 1, 63).

52 *Summa Theologica*, 1, qu. xiii.

53 There is a lucid summary, to which I am indebted, in R. P. Phillips,
Modern Thomistic Philosophy (London 1935) 11, 166–73.

54 'Es el sujeto sobre quien se discurre y pondera ... uno como centro,
de quien reparte el discurso, líneas de ponderación y sutileza a las
entidades que lo rodean; esto es, a los adjuntos que lo coronan,
como son sus causas, sus efectos, atributos, calidades, conting-
encias, circunstancias de tiempo, lugar, modo, etc., y cualquiera
otro término correspondiente; valos careando de uno en uno con
el sujeto, y unos con otros, entre sí; y en descubriendo alguna
conformidad y conveniencia, que digan, ya con el principal sujeto,
ya unos con otros, exprímela, pondérala y en esto está la sutileza ...
De suerte, que, esta primera especie de concepto consiste en una
cierta armonía y agradable correspondencia, que dicen entre sí los
términos, o con el sujeto . . . Cuando esta correspondencia está
recóndita, y que es menester discurrir para observarla, es más sutil,

cuanto más cuesta ... este modo de concepto se llama proporcional, proque en él se atiende a la correspondencia que hacen los extremos cognoscibles entre sí' (*Agudeza*, Disc. iv; I, 64, 65, 66).

55 'Fórmase por artificio contrapuesto a la proporción'. 'Allí se busca la correspondencia; aquí, al contrario, la oposición entre los extremos.' 'Nace de la proporción la hermosura, no siempre de la improporción en el hecho; pero el notarla en el concepto es perfección.' 'Es muy platicada esta disonancia por lo fácil del concebirla.' 'Cuando es mayor la repugnancia, hace más conceptuosa la improporción.' 'La mezcla de proporción y improporción hace una armonía agradable.' (*Agudeza*, Disc. v; I, 74, 75, 76, 84, 86).

56 'Fue este culto poeta cisne en los concentos, águila en los conceptos; en toda especie de agudeza eminente, pero en ésta de contraproporciones consistió el triunfo de su grande ingenio: vense sus obras entretejidas desta sutileza' (ibid., 79).

57 Góngora's predilection for this type of metaphor is of course due to the fact that it enables him to express the likeness (proportion) and unlikeness (disproportion) of his analogies at the same time: the rock is a lighthouse and a watchtower by its size and position, but it cannot in fact be either because there is no light and no warning sound.

58 E. Sarmiento, op. cit., 290.

59 Matter and form are here used in their Aristotelian–Scholastic sense, form being that which determines matter by giving a thing its definite character. The soul, for instance, is the form of the body. The 'form' of style is thus the intellectual content, which gives their meaning to the words and sentences that communicate the content.

60 Aristarchus of Samothrace (c. 217–145 B.C.), Greek grammarian and textual critic, who held that a poet should be interpreted by his own usage, and who thus avoided allegorical interpretations.

61 Cf. Góngora's defence of his poetry quoted above (pp. 16–17), based on the 'mysteriousness' that should impel the reader to dig below the surface.

62 *Agudeza*, Disc. lx; II, 228–30, 235. The concluding sentence leads on to the discussion 'Of the Variety of Styles'. Because of the length of this quotation the Spanish text is omitted.

63 '[La versabilità] pon l'una in luogo dell'altra, come i giocolieri i lor calcoli. E questa è la metafora, madre delle poesie, de' simboli e delle imprese. E quegli è più ingegnoso, che può conoscere e accoppiar circonstanze più lontane, come diremo.' (*Il cannochiale aristotelico*, in *Trattatisti e narratori del Seicento*, ed. Ezio Raimondi [La Letteratura Italiana: Storia e Testi, vol. XXXVI], 32. This

volume also contains selections from the works of Peregrini and Sforza Pallavicino. There is a modern facsimile of the Turin 1670 edition of *Il cannochiale aristotelico*, with an Introduction by August Buck, in the series *Ars Poetica*. *Texte und Studien zur Dichtungslehre und Dichtkunst*, vol. v (Berlin–Zurich 1968).

64 'Ed eccoci alla fin pervenuti grado per grado al più alto colmo delle figure ingegnose, a paragon delle quali tutte le altre figure fin qui recitate perdono il pregio, essendo la metafora il più ingegnoso e acuto, il più pellegrino e mirabile, il più gioviale e giovevole, il più facondo e fecondo parto dell'umano intelletto' (ed. cit., 73).

65 'Vengo alle simboliche arguzie della Natura, oltre ogni credenza ingegnosissime, e degne di ammirazione anco a' filosofi . . . sapientissima nelle cose necessariamente ordinate alla publica utilità, così nelle cose piacevoli si studia per mera pompa d'ingegno di mostrarsi arguta e faceta. E che è questa varietà de' fiori, altri spinosi e irsuti, altri morbidi e dilicati . . . in varie vezzosissime guise raccolti, rivolti, sparti, acuti, globosi, scanalati, piani, stellati; parendo che il sol nascente, per far della terra un cielo, scuota le stelle di cielo in terra. Tutte queste, oltra mill'altre, son pur figure eleganti e vivaci arguzie dell'ingegnosa Natura . . . poichè la Natura istessa allora scherza e frasezzia con mille arguti e ingegnosi concetti' (ed. cit., 26–7).

66 Tesauro's principal contribution to the theory of Wit concerns what Gracián calls the 'Wit of ratiocination' (Disc.iii). Two discourses (xxxvi and xxxvii) are dedicated to one form of this, *argumentos conceptuosos*. He stresses, of course, that witty arguments aim at beauty not logic, but it was Tesauro who analysed such arguments as 'urbanely fallacious' enthymemes. This form of Wit is not dealt with here, for although Góngora has examples of such arguments among his poems, there are none in *Polifemo*. For this aspect of Tesauro's treatise see S. L. Bethell, 'Gracián, Tesauro and the Nature of Metaphysical Wit', in *The Northern Miscellany of Literary Criticism*, no. 1 (1953) 30–2.

67 *Soledades*, I, 294–6.

68 Góngora's contemporaries, whether favourably or unfavourably inclined to his major poems, stressed his *conceptismo*. Juan de Jáuregui, poet, critic and painter, sent Góngora in 1614 an 'Antidote for the pestilential poetry of the *Solitudes*, applied to their author to protect him from himself'. Góngora, he contended, was not born to be a poet because he has no natural talent and has not made good this lack by study and technical application; on the other hand, let him continue to express his *conceptos* and his *agudeza* for in that sphere Jáuregui confessed himself surpassed. Pedro

Díaz de Rivas, in his 'Apologetic Discourses' on *Polifemo* and *Soledades* (written before 1618) affirmed that the reason why Góngora was sometimes more obscure than Virgil was because he aspired on these occasions to greater *agudeza* in his thought. See Eunice J. Gates, *Documentos gongorinos* (Mexico 1960) 85, 62. In contrast to the seventeenth-century stressing of Wit modern critics have stressed only Góngora's *culteranismo*. Not till 1961 did anyone suggest that *Polifemo* was also a *conceptista* poem: Elias J. Rivers, 'El conceptismo del *Polifemo*', in *Atenea* (Concepción, Chile), vol. CXLIII (1961) 102–9.

69 'No oscuridad: claridad radiante, claridad deslumbrante. Claridad de íntima, profunda iluminación. Mar luciente: cristal azul. Cielo color zafiro, sin mácula, constelado de diamantes, o rasgado por la corva carrera del sol. *Mundo abreviado, renovado y puro*, entre las armonías de lo blanco, lo rojo y lo verde. Mundo iluminado, ya no sólo por la luz del día, sino por una irradiación, una luz interior, una como fosforescencia de todas las cosas. *Claritas*. Hiperluminosidad. Luz estética: clara por bella, bella por clara.' (*Soledades de Góngora*, editadas por Dámaso Alonso, Madrid 1927, 35–6.) The previous quotation from Gerald Brenan comes from *The Literature of the Spanish People*, 2nd ed. (Cambridge 1953) 236.

70 Walther Pabst, 'Góngoras Schöpfung in seinen Gedichten *Polifemo* und *Soledades*', in *Revue Hispanique*, LXXX (1930) 138–9. There is a Spanish translation, *La creación gongorina en los poemas Polifemo y Soledades* (Madrid 1966).

71 'Góngora ist viel naiver als andere Menschen, vor Allem viel naiver als seine Leser. Denn—wer in aller Welt ist naiver als der Impressionist? Der Impressionist ist der zum Sinnenzustand des Kindes zurückgekehrte Mensch. In Spanien aber gibt es keinen grösseren Impressionisten als Góngora ... niemand hat den Impressionismus mit solcher Konsequenz, mit so anhaltender Unbefangenheit der Sinne durchgeführt wie Góngora. Wenn seine Sinne Nahrung erhalten, rauben si ihr die Perspektive' (op. cit., 141).

72 In its first stage or version this appeared in 1950 as 'Monstruosidad y belleza en el Polifemo de Góngora', in *Poesía española. Ensayo de métodos y límites estilísticos* (5th. ed., Madrid 1966) 315–92. This was reworked into an edition with commentary which formed the second volume of *Góngora y el Polifemo* (Madrid 1960). This work was amplified in subsequent editions until in the fifth (Madrid 1967) it became 3 vols. Text and commentary comprise the third.

73 '¡Qué chasco se habría llevado Paul Verlaine y los simbolistas franceses y nuestros modernistas, si hubieran podido conocer las leyes de lógica y trabadísima sustentación del sistema gongorino!

Nada de desenfreno, nada de nebulosidad, nada de impresionismo: implacable rigor, exquisito orden' (*Poesía española*, ed. cit., 334).

74 'Lo sereno y lo atormentado; lo lumínico y lo lóbrego; la suavidad y lo áspero; la gracia y la esquiveza y los terribles deseos reprimidos. Eterno femenino y eterno masculino, que forman toda la contraposición, la pugna, el claroscuro del Barroco. En una obra de Góngora se condensaron de tal modo, que es en sí ella misma como una abreviatura de toda la complejidad de aquel mundo y de lo que en él fermentaba. Sí, se condensaron—luz y sombra, norma e ímpetu, gracia y malaugurio—en la *Fábula de Polifemo*, que es, por esta causa, la obra más representativa del Barroco europeo. 'Pero esto es lo asombroso: Galatea y Polifemo (lo celestial y lo telúrico) se resolvieron—estéticamente—en un organismo único: en esa *Fábula de Polifemo y Galatea*, ya unidad, ya eterna criatura de arte. Prodigio de arte' (op. cit., 392).

75 Robert Jammes, *Études sur l'oeuvre poétique de Don Luis de Góngora y Argote* (Bordeaux 1967) 546–7.

76 *Poems of Góngora Selected, Introduced and Annotated by R. O. Jones* (Cambridge 1966) 36–7. The same point had been made about the *Polifemo* in Jones's earlier study, 'Neoplatonism and the *Soledades*', in *Bulletin of Hispanic Studies*, XL (1963) 14–15.

77 C. Colin Smith, 'An Approach to Góngora's *Polifemo*', in *Bulletin of Hispanic Studies*, XLII (1965) 230–1, 236, 238.

78 The most extreme form of this fallacy is to be found in the most recent book on the poet, *Luis de Góngora*, by David William Foster and Virginia Ramos Foster, Twayne's World Authors Series no. 266 (New York 1973). They are over-much influenced by the marxist-oriented study of Robert Jammes, already mentioned, which detected 'a persistent fluctuation in the poet's work between adherence to accepted themes and forms . . . and a deviation from accepted norms in his poetry which was antiestablishment in both form . . . and theme' (p. 97). In consequence their laboured analysis of *Polifemo* finds a dualism. On the one hand there is a forward-looking 'amoralism' and a 'blatantly anti-Christian theme'; on the other hand there is the retrograde utilization of a traditional myth by a poet who shows a 'general iconoclastic stance towards literary tradition' (pp. 100–3). None-the-less, they conclude, the poem, in the triumph of its artistry, does 'suggest a way out of the bleakness of the contemporary Counter-Reformation world' (p. 161). Such views indicate a disregard of literary theory and literary and cultural history (not to speak of ideological prejudices, which do not really help to interpret the literature of the past). Góngora was not alone in being 'iconoclastic' (in the sense of satirical-burlesque):

this is a widespread characteristic of Spanish literature, in both verse and prose, from about 1590. But poets observed the theory of the Three Styles; when they wanted to be 'iconoclastic' they wrote in the Low Style (here considered forward-looking), but when they wanted to write in the High Style (here considered retrograde) they sang of the beauty of Nature, or of Ideal Love, or they retold the story of Polyphemus and Galatea and of countless other myths. (For the thematic and chronological range of this mythological poetry in Spain see José M. de Cossío, *Fábulas mitológicas en España* [Madrid 1952].) From the time of the Renaissance a Christian education was a classical education, and it remained so until the emergence in our own day of literary critics who would seem to have known neither. Boys learned their catechism and studied Virgil and Ovid. If the classical myths are anti-Christian, how was it that Calderón, whose Christian beliefs have not yet been called in question, wrote eight *autos sacramentales* in which mythology provided allegories for Christian dogmas, and seventeen palace plays and operas in which myths and mythological legends offered dramatic plots for the presentation of various aspects of human psychology and experience, with no more mention of Christian beliefs than there is in *Polifemo*?

79 'Así don Luis de Góngora, en su aliñado, elocuente y recóndito poema del *Polifemo*...' (*Agudeza*, Disc. xlviii; 11, 149).

80 *Góngora y el Polifemo*, ed. cit., 1, 186–207.

81 op. cit., 538–47.

82 Perhaps the best of the many general works on this theme is the concise account by Peter V. Marinelli, *Pastoral* (*The Critical Idiom*, no. 15, London 1971).

83 C. Colin Smith, op. cit., 234–5. See also 221–2.

84 Hesiod, *Works and Days* (lines 109–201); Virgil, *Aeneid*, VIII, 313–25, and the *Fourth Eclogue*; Ovid, *Metamorphoses*, I, 89–112. See Harry Levin, *The Myth of the Golden Age in the Renaissance* (Bloomington and London 1969).

85 One of the examples (for which our modern taste must make allowances) of the application of this type of Wit provided by Gracián as illustration is a sermon preached on the 'dormition' and 'assumption' of the Virgin Mary. She was described as dying in flames (of love) in order, through the allusion to the Phoenix, to facilitate the transition to rebirth in her physical assumption into heaven. (*Agudeza*, Disc. lix; 11, 222–3).

86 Two examples from Góngora by way of illustration. The western ocean is 'la que sella/cerúlea tumba fría/las cenizas del día' (the cold, blue tomb that seals the ashes of the day: *Soledades*, 1, 390–

92). A fisherman lover refers thus to the passion he already felt as a boy for his lady: 'cuando de tus dos soles/fulminado, ya señas no ligeras/de mis cenizas dieron tus riberas' (when I having been set on fire by your two suns, your shores already showed the signs of my ashes; ibid., 11, 560–62).

87 Lucan, *De bello civili*, I, 456. Horace, *Odes*, I, iv, 13.

88 Antonio Vilanova, *Las fuentes y los temas del Polifemo de Góngora* (Madrid 1957) I, 332–53.

89 Baltasar del Alcázar (1530–1606) refers to Death as 'Aquella horrible y pálida figura / que nunca supo perdonar ni sabe' (*Poesías*, ed. Real Academia Española [Madrid 1910] 202). Calderón, in *El pleito matrimonial del cuerpo y el alma*, calls Death 'Pálida Muerte' (line 17), and in *La cena de Baltasar* makes Death send King Belshazzar a reminder of himself in the form of sleep, 'mi imagen pálida, el sueño', and the king refers to the dream within this sleep as 'el pálido sueño' (lines 987, 1197).

90 See Vilanova, op. cit., I, 332–53.

91 *Poesía española*, ed. cit., 325–32; *Góngora y el Polifemo*, ed. cit., III, 61–3.

92 Vilanova finds the source for the description of Polyphemus (lines 57–64) in Virgil's description of Atlas in *Aeneid*, IV, 246–51, stating that it contains nearly all the characteristic features of the Góngora passage (op. cit., I, 469–71). But the essential element—the *conceptista* correspondence of the hair with the River Lethe—is not in Virgil.

93 *Poesía española*, ed. cit., 374–6; *Góngora y el Polifemo*, ed. cit., 99–100.

94 There are two elements in the image, one from classical, the other from Petrarchan sources. The Dog Star 'barks' in the sun, according to Góngora's early commentators, either because it is belching flames, or because of heat and thirst. Vilanova quotes the source, given by Salcedo Coronel, in Book v of the *Astronomica* of Manillius: 'Exoriturque canis, latratque canicula flamma', etc. (op. cit., 11, 54). Joseph Pellicer gives further examples: 'emittens calidum latratum' in Nonius Marcellus; 'calidum latrauit Scirius astro' in Statius (*Lecciones solemnes a las obras de don Luis de Góngora* [Madrid 1630] col. 182). There is nothing in these examples to connect the Dog with the passion of love. Góngora makes the connexion by transforming it into the salamander. This had become in the sixteenth century a traditional image for a lover, deriving from Petrarch. (See examples in Vilanova, 11, 48–51). There is no recorded source for Góngora's connexion of the salamander with the barking dog.

95 'Crystal', originally a Petrarchan metaphor for tears, came to denote the translucent quality of a woman's fine skin, through which the veins show. Góngora uses it frequently in his poems; here, for example, in lines 103, 243, 328 and 353.

96 Ovid, as generally interpreted, makes him the son of Faunus himself (i.e. Pan), 'Acis erat Fauno nymphaque Symaethide cretus', but this could, of course, be equally understood as 'a faun'.

97 For violas and their colours in Latin, Italian and Spanish poetry see Vilanova, op. cit., II, 371–7.

98 Colin Smith, who sees Galatea as 'a fertility-figure whose unformalized worship is partly erotic, partly spiritual', and who sees the poem as 'showing man as a part of the animal world and living in sensible harmony with the rest of Nature', reacts as follows to the description of the lovers' union: 'The love-making of Acis and Galathea [lines 321–36] has no emotional content, and it is even performed without a word being spoken. There is a fine biological beauty about it, a sort of animal simplicity and a Lawrentian purity' (op. cit., 222, 236). He then quotes García Lorca, who, he says, 'saw this with wonderful clarity': 'It can be said that the poem has a floral sexuality. A sexuality of stamen and pistil in the moving spring-time process of pollen becoming airborne.' (Translated from 'La imagen poética de Góngora', in *Obras completas* 3rd ed. [Madrid 1957] 83.) Other readers may find the poetic expression, here as well as in the preceding stanzas, too sophisticatedly refined to convey this biological simplicity.

99 From the famous elegy 'On the Death of his Father'. Manrique's dates are 1440?–1478. Pellicer adds as a further parallel (less apposite than the passage from Ecclesiastes) the saying of Heraclitus 'all ages pass away, like running water' (*Lecciones solemnes*, ad loc.).

100 See the numerous passages quoted by Cornelius a Lapide (Cornelis Cornelissen van den Steen) in his *Commentaria in Scripturam Sacram* of 1614 (edition of Lyons and Paris, 1865, vol. IV, p. 40 ff.).

101 Francisco de Quevedo, *Obra poética*, ed. José Manuel Blecua (Madrid 1969) I, 185.

102 E.g. Mircea Eliade, *Images et symboles* (Paris 1952). I quote from the English translation, *Images and Symbols* (Search Book: New York 1961): 'The Waters symbolise the entire universe of the virtual; they are the *fons et origo*, the reservoir of all the potentialities of existence; they *precede* every form and *sustain* every creation. The exemplary image of the whole creation is the Island that suddenly 'manifests' itself amidst the waves. Conversely, immersion in the waters symbolises a regression into the pre-formal,

reintegration into the undifferentiated mode of pre-existence. Emergence repeats the cosmogonic act of formal manifestation; while immersion is equivalent to a dissolution of forms. That is why the symbolism of the Waters includes Death as well as Re-Birth' (p. 150). 'Everything that has form manifests itself above the Waters, by detaching itself from them. On the other hand, as soon as it is separated from the waters and has ceased to be potential (virtual), every form comes under the laws of Time and of Life; it acquires limitations, participates in the universal becoming, is subject to history, decays away and is finally emptied of substance unless it be regenerated by periodic immersions in the Waters, repetitions of the 'deluge' with its cosmogonic corollary. . . . The 'Waters of Death', for example, reveal their profound meaning only to the degree that one knows the structure of the aquatic symbolism' (pp. 152–3).

103 As will have been apparent from the numerous conceits analysed in this Introduction, a constant feature of the imagery of *Polifemo* is the metaphorical movement in either direction between the human and the animal and vegetable worlds, and between the human and the inanimate: trees in front of the Giant's cave are a garrison and their foliage is matted hair; his cave is a yawn, he himself a mountain, his eye a sun, his hair a river and his beard a torrent; Galatea is crystal rock, crystal water, a peacock, a swan, jasmine and lilies, etc. Colin Smith lists nearly all these equivalences, and sees them as effecting the 'merging of the human and semi-human figures with the natural scene' and 'of lower forms of animal life with the plant life and with other phenomena'. He sees the purpose of this as pastoral, i.e. as portraying 'man living in proximity to, and in harmony with, Nature', and as portraying the process by which 'the poet tries to make us see the oneness of creation'. But, on a deeper level, he also sees it as exemplifying 'the starkness and primitiveness of the *Polifemo*, in which the processes of landscape-formation and species-creation are still going on' (op. cit., 222, 227, 229, 235). This 'evolutionary' vision is of course modern. 'The oneness of creation' was at the root of the Poetic of Correspondence, and these metaphorical transferences are the basis of the poetic Wit it gave rise to. It has been the purpose of this Introduction to show that *Polifemo* exemplifies this Wit. This sufficiently accounts for the imagery without our having to glimpse a near-philosophical view of Nature.

104 The Neoplatonism of Polifemo was first argued as an appendage to R. O. Jones's article on 'Neoplatonism and the Soledades', in *Bulletin of Hispanic Studies*, XL (1963) 14–15. The starting-point for

this study was the misinterpretation of Góngora's statement that beneath the surface of his verse there could be found a 'mystery' (see above, p.93). Colin Smith asked some telling questions on the Neoplatonism of *Polifemo* (op. cit., 235-7), which were not very satisfactorily answered in Jones's rejoinder, 'Góngora and Neoplatonism Again' (*Bulletin of Hispanic Studies*, XLIII [1966] 117-20).

105 This is *Epístola VI* in Elias L. Rivers's edition of Aldana's *Poesías* (*Clásicos Castellanos*, no. 143, Madrid 1966) 57-74. The poem is also published in Arthur Terry's *An Anthology of Spanish Poetry* (Pergamon Press, Oxford 1965), vol. I, 113-25.

106 Not only *passim* in the works already referred to on many occasions but especially in the following: 'La simetría bilateral', in *Estudios y ensayos gongorinos* (Madrid 1953) 117-73.

107 In *Revista de Filología Española*, XLIV (1961) 139-66.

108 'Rich Rhyme in Góngora's *Polifemo*', in *Bulletin of Hispanic Studies*, XLII (1965) 106-12.

109 op. cit., 112.

After the proofs of this book were corrected there came to my notice *The Baroque Poem, A Comparative Survey*, by Harold B. Segel (E. P. Dutton, New York 1974). It contains an anthology of poems in twelve languages, with English translations. Its introductory survey of baroque poetry is original and valuable in that it covers both Eastern and Western Europe. The account of poetic theory and style is, however, conventional.

III

*The Fable of
Polyphemus and Galatea.
The Texts*

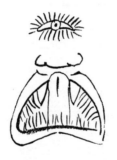

1

ESTAS QUE ME dictó rimas sonoras,
culta sí, aunque bucólica, Talía
—¡oh excelso conde!—, en las purpúreas horas
que es rosas la alba y rosicler el día,
ahora que de luz tu Niebla doras,   *5*
escucha, al son de la zampoña mía,
si ya los muros no te ven, de Huelva,
peinar el viento, fatigar la selva.

2

Templado, pula en la maestra mano
el generoso pájaro su pluma,   *10*
o tan mudo en la alcándara, que en vano
aun desmentir al cascabel presuma;
tascando haga el freno de oro, cano,
del caballo andaluz la ociosa espuma;
gima el lebrel en el cordón de seda.   *15*
Y al cuerno, al fin, la cítara suceda.

3

Treguas al ejercicio sean robusto,
ocio atento, silencio dulce, en cuanto
debajo escuchas de dosel augusto,
del músico jayán el fiero canto.   *20*
Alterna con las Musas hoy el gusto;
que si la mía puede ofrecer tanto
clarín (y de la Fama no segundo),
tu nombre oirán los términos del mundo.

(108)

1

THESE SOUNDING RHYMES Thalia bids me write,
Most noble count, a rude yet cultured Muse,
In these purpureal hours when dawn is bright
With rose and morning breaks in roseate hues,
Hear, since Niebla's cloud you gild with light,   *5*
Nor to my rustic pipe your ear refuse
If, watched by Huelva's towers, with hawks and hounds
You scour the air or beat the forest's bounds.

2

Though ready, let the noble hawk remain
Polishing, on the wrist, each lordly plume,   *10*
Or, silent on his perch, although in vain,
To hush the witness of his bell presume;
The Andalusian steed, biting the rein,
Whiten his golden bit with idle spume;
The greyhound whine against his silken lead;   *15*
And to the horn the zither's notes succeed.

3

With gentle silence and attentive leisure
At truce with strenuous sports, listen in state
From your high seat, while now the barbarous measure
Of the gigantic bard I celebrate.   *20*
Turn to the Muses this day for your pleasure,
For mine may surely offer such a great
Clarion (which yields no higher place to Fame),
That earth's most distant bounds shall hear your name.

(109)

4

Donde espumoso el mar sicilïano   25
el pie argenta de plata al Lilibeo
(bóveda o de las fraguas de Vulcano,
o tumba de los huesos de Tifeo),
pálidas señas cenizoso un llano
—cuando no del sacrílego deseo—   30
del duro oficio da. Allí una alta roca
mordaza es a una gruta, de su boca.

5

Guarnición tosca de este escollo duro
troncos robustos son, a cuya greña
menos luz debe, menos aire puro   35
la caverna profunda, que a la peña;
caliginoso lecho, el seno obscuro
ser de la negra noche nos lo enseña
infame turba de nocturnas aves,
gimiendo tristes y volando graves.   40

6

De este, pues, formidable de la tierra
bostezo, el melancólico vacío
a Polifemo, horror de aquella sierra,
bárbara choza es, albergue umbrío
y redil espacioso donde encierra   45
cuanto las cumbres ásperas cabrío,
de los montes, esconde: copia bella
que un silbo junta y un peñasco sella.

7

Un monte era de miembros eminente
este (que, de Neptuno hijo fiero,   50
de un ojo ilustra el orbe de su frente,
émulo casi del mayor lucero)
cíclope, a quien el pino más valiente,
bastón, le obedecía, tan ligero,
y al grave peso junco tan delgado,   55
que un día era bastón y otro cayado.

4

Where, as it treads on the Sicilian surge,   *25*
Marsala's foot is shod with silver foam
(Either a vault that houses Vulcan's forge,
Or serves the bones of Typhon for a tomb)
Upon an ashy plain pale signs emerge
From this one's sacrilegious wish, or from   *30*
The other's toil, and there a lofty rock
Muzzles a cave, whose mouth it seems to block.

5

For garniture some rugged tree-trunks grow
Round this hard boulder, to whose matted hair
Even less the cave's recesses seem to owe   *35*
Than to the rock for light and purer air;
Above the murky den, as if to show
What black and midnight depths are hidden there,
A flock of nightly birds defiles the skies
With ponderous wings and melancholy cries.   *40*

6

Earth, yawning hugely, leaves a dismal space
Which makes the terror of the countryside,
The Cyclops, a barbaric dwelling-place,
A sombre shelter and a pinfold wide
In which as many of the caprine race   *45*
He may enclose as with their numbers hide
The rugged mountains, and whose comely flocks
A whistle gathers and a boulder locks.

7

Of human limbs a lofty mountain made
The Cyclops seemed, Poseidon's savage son,   *50*
The broad horizon of whose brow displayed
A single eye, the rival of the sun;
Like a light staff the stoutest pine obeyed
His mighty grasp, but if he leaned thereon
Under his weight, a crumpled reed, it shook,   *55*
One day a staff, the next a shepherd's crook.

8

Negro el cabello, imitador undoso
de las obscuras aguas del Leteo,
al viento que lo peina proceloso,
vuela sin orden, pende sin aseo;   60
un torrente es su barba impetüoso,
que (adusto hijo de este Pirineo)
su pecho inunda, o tarde, o mal, o en vano
surcada aun de los dedos de su mano.

9

No la Trinacria en sus montañas, fiera   65
armó de crüeldad, calzó de viento,
que redima feroz, salve ligera,
su piel manchada de colores ciento:
pellico es ya la que en los bosques era
mortal horror al que con paso lento   70
los bueyes a su albergue reducía,
pisando la dudosa luz del día.

10

Cercado es (cuanto más capaz, más lleno)
de la fruta, el zurrón, casi abortada,
que el tardo otoño deja al blando seno   75
de la piadosa hierba, encomendada:
la serba, a quien le da rugas el heno;
la pera, de quien fue cuna dorada
la rubia paja, y—pálida tutora—
la niega avara, y pródiga la dora.   80

11

Erizo es el zurrón, de la castaña,
y (entre el membrillo o verde o datilado)
de la manzana hipócrita, que engaña,
a lo pálido no, a lo arrebolado,
y, de la encina (honor de la montaña,   85
que pabellón al siglo fue dorado)
el tributo, alimento, aunque grosero,
del mejor mundo, del candor primero.

(112)

8

His hair, which curls in raven tresses, seems
To rival Lethe's dark obscurities;
Unkempt it hangs or in disorder streams
Under the comb of the tempestuous breeze;   60
His beard like an impetuous torrent teems,
Swarthy as fits its parent Pyrenees,
Flooding his breast, and barbered, late or ill,
By a prodigious hand with puny skill.

9

No savage beast Trinacria's mountains breed,   65
Shod with the wind and armed with cruel hate,
Can save with violence or redeem with speed
Its skin with many colours maculate:
To make the giant's cloak the woods must cede
The mortal fear of him who, plodding late   70
To drive his cattle on their homeward way,
Treads the uncertain light of dying day.

10

His wallet, ever full however wide,
Like a scarce ripened orchard has compressed
Such fruits as tardy autumn must confide   75
To pitying grasses for a kindly breast:
Sorbs that in hay mature their wrinkled hide,
Pears that in saffron straw are laid to rest—
Pale guardians these, who miserly withhold
Their charge from sight, yet prodigal of gold.   80

11

Husk is the wallet of the chestnut too
And (mixed with quinces, brown like dates, or green)
The apple, hypocrite, whose outward hue
Cheats not with pallor but with crimson sheen,
And, of the oak (pride of the mountain, who   85
The shelter of the golden age has been),
That gift which once, though rude, sufficed to feed
The primal candour of a purer breed.

12
Cera y cáñamo unió (que no debiera)
cien cañas, cuyo bárbaro rüído,   90
de más ecos que unió cánamo y cera
albogues, duramente es repetido.
La selva se confunde, el mar se altera,
rompe Tritón su caracol torcido,
sordo huye el bajel a vela y remo: 95
¡tal la música es de Polifemo!

13
Ninfa, de Doris hija, la más bella,
adora, que vio el reino de la espuma.
Galatea es su nombre, y dulce en ella
el terno Venus de sus Gracias suma.   100
Son una y otra luminosa estrella
lucientes ojos de su blanca pluma:
si roca de cristal no es de Neptuno,
pavón de Venus es, cisne de Juno.

14
Purpúreas rosas sobre Galatea   105
la Alba entre lilios cándidos deshoja:
duda el Amor cuál más su color sea,
o púrpura nevada, o nieve roja.
De su frente la perla es, eritrea,
émula vana. El ciego dios se enoja,   110
y, condenado su esplendor, la deja
pender en oro al nácar de su oreja.

15
Invidia de las ninfas y cuidado
de cuantas honra el mar deidades era;
pompa del marinero niño alado   115
que sin fanal conduce su venera.
Verde el cabello, el pecho no escamado,
ronco sí, escucha a Glauco la ribera
inducir a pisar la bella ingrata,
en carro de cristal, campos de plata.   120

12

A hundred pipes with wax and string are joined
(A horrid din the vile contrivance makes);   *90*
As many echoes as the pipes combined
By string and wax the raucous music wakes.
The tree-tops toss, the surges crash and grind,
His trump of twisted nacre Triton breaks,
Fear wings with sail or oar the deafened boats: *95*
So barbarous are Polyphemus' notes!

13

He loves a nymph, daughter of Doris, fair
Above all seen in Ocean's kingdom yet;
Her name is Galatea, and in her
Of Venus' Graces all the charms are met.   *100*
Bright stars, both one and other, are the pair
Of shining eyes in snow-white plumage set:
If not a rock of crystal in the sea,
Then Juno's swan or Venus' peacock she.

14

Encrimsoned roses mixed with lilies white   *105*
On Galatea's beauty Dawn bestows,
Till Love can hardly tell her hue aright,
Whether a rosy snow or snowy rose.
The Abyssinian pearl is scarcely white
Against her brow, and now its splendour glows,   *110*
Condemned by scornful Cupid, as a mere
Trinket in gold, hung from her shell-like ear.

15

Envy of other nymphs and amorous care
Of every ocean-honoured god as well,
Pride of the winged and youthful mariner   *115*
Who, lacking eyes, yet steers his mother's shell.
Glaucus, with scaleless breast and sea-green hair
Is heard, hoarse-voiced, by every shore to tell
His love, and beg the thankless nymph to ride
His crystal car across the silver tide.   *120*

(115)

16

Marino joven, las cerúleas sienes,
del más tierno coral ciñe Palemo,
rico de cuantos la agua engendra bienes,
del Faro odioso al promontorio extremo;
mas en la gracia igual, si en los desdenes   *125*
perdonado algo más que Polifemo,
de la que, aún no le oyó, y, calzada plumas,
tantas flores pisó como él espumas.

17

Huye la ninfa bella; y el marino
amante nadador, ser bien quisiera,   *130*
ya que no áspid a su pie divino,
dorado pomo a su veloz carrera;
mas, ¿cuál diente mortal, cuál metal fino
la fuga suspender podrá ligera
que el desdén solicita? ¡Oh cuánto yerra   *135*
delfín que sigue en agua corza en tierra!

18

Sicilia, en cuanto oculta, en cuanto ofrece,
copa es de Baco, huerto de Pomona:
tanto de frutas ésta la enriquece,
cuanto aquél de racimos la corona.   *140*
En carro que estival trillo parece,
a sus campañas Ceres no perdona,
de cuyas siempre fértiles espigas
las provincias de Europa son hormigas.

19

A Pales su viciosa cumbre debe   *145*
lo que a Ceres, y aún más, su vega llana;
pues si en la una granos de oro llueve,
copos nieva en la otra mil de lana.
De cuantos siegan oro, esquilan nieve,
o en pipas guardan la exprimida grana,   *150*
bien sea religión, bien amor sea,
deidad, aunque sin templo, es Galatea.

16

Palaemon, young sea-god, though he adorn
With clearest coral his cerulean locks,
Rich in all goods which of the sea are born
From hateful Pharos to Messina's rocks,
Gains no more grace, if something less of scorn,   *125*
Than Polyphemus, for she only mocks
His suit, and fleeing, shod with feathers, leaves
The flowers behind as fast as he the waves.

17

The fair nymph flees, and swimming in pursuit
Her sea-born lover follows, eager less   *130*
To be an aspic to her sacred foot
Than a gold apple to her rapid race.
But ah, what fatal tooth, what glittering fruit
Avails to stay the flying maiden's pace
Whom scorn impels. The dolphin strives in vain   *135*
To match by sea the deer that runs the plain.

18

Pomona's wealth Trinacria displays,
And hides as plentifully Bacchus' spoil;
The fruit of one hangs heavy on her trees
As round her brow the other's clusters coil.   *140*
Ceres, her car a threshing-mill, decrees
No respite to the produce of her soil,
While from her fertile granary, like ants,
The lands of Europe satisfy their wants.

19

To Pales more her teeming upland owes   *145*
Even than to Ceres her more level plain;
A thousand woolly snowflakes one bestows
To match the other's showers of golden grain;
And all who reap the gold or shear the snows,
Or purple juice from press to wine-cask strain,   *150*
For love or worship, shrineless though she be,
Take Galatea for their deity.

20

Sin aras, no: que el margen donde para
del espumoso mar su pie ligero,
al labrador, de sus primicias ara,   155
de sus esquilmos es al ganadero;
de la Copia—a la tierra, poco avara—
el cuerno vierte el hortelano, entero,
sobre la mimbre que tejió, prolija,
si artificiosa no, su honesta hija.   160

21

Arde la juventud, y los arados
peinan las tierras que surcaron antes,
mal conducidos, cuando no arrastrados
de tardos bueyes, cual su dueño errantes;
sin pastor que los silbe, los ganados   165
los crujidos ignoran resonantes,
de las hondas, si, en vez del pastor pobre,
el céfiro no silba, o cruje el robre.

22

Mudo la noche el can, el día, dormido,
de cerro en cerro y sombra en sombra yace.   170
Bala el ganado; al mísero balido,
nocturno el lobo de las sombras nace.
Cébase; y fiero, deja humedecido
en sangre de una lo que la otra pace.
¡ Revoca, Amor, los silbos, o a su dueño.   175
el silencio del can siga, y el sueño!

23

La fugitiva ninfa, en tanto, donde
hurta un laurel su tronco al sol ardiente,
tantos jazmines cuanta hierba esconde
la nieve de sus miembros, da a una fuente.   180
Dulce se queja, dulce le responde
un ruiseñor a otro, y dulcemente
al sueño da sus ojos la armonía,
por no abrasar con tres soles el día.

(118)

20

Shrineless, but yet she has an altar where
Her light step pauses by the foaming sea,
On which both herd and ploughman offer her   155
The tithes and firstfruits of their industry;
Grudged nothing by the soil, the gardener
Empties his horn of plenty liberally
Into the osier which, though ill designed,
With no small toil his worthy daughter twined.   160

21

Youth is on fire, and while the ploughman's share
Scratches the soil instead of furrowing,
Ill-drawn or worse, behind a lazy pair
Of bullocks, like their master wandering,
The sheep, to whom no shepherd whistles, hear   165
No more the crack of the resounding sling,
Or, to replace the humble herd they lack,
The breezes whistle and the oak-twigs crack.

22

The sheepdog, mute by night, slumbers by day,
Skulking from mound to mound, from shade to shade,   170
While on his charges, bleating in dismay,
Nocturnal wolves steal from the shadowy glade.
The wild beasts thrive, leaving their mangled prey
To stain with blood the grass where others feed.
Restore the whistles, Love, or like the vanished   175
Herds let the dog's silence and sleep be banished!

23

The flying maiden pauses by a spring
From noontide's blaze spared by a laurel tree,
Her snowy limbs no fewer scattering
Of jasmines than they hide of greenery.   180
Sweetly complaining, sweetly answering,
The songbirds with their mingled harmony
Bring slumber no less sweetly to her eyes,
For fear a triple sun should scorch the skies.

24

Salamandria del Sol, vestido estrellas,   *185*
latiendo el Can del cielo estaba, cuando
(polvo el cabello, húmidas centellas,
si no ardientes aljófares, sudando)
llegó Acis; y, de ambas luces bellas
dulce Occidente viendo al sueño blando,   *190*
su boca dio, y sus ojos cuanto pudo,
al sonoro cristal, al cristal mudo.

25

Era Acis un venablo de Cupido,
de un fauno, medio hombre, medio fiera,
en Simetis, hermosa ninfa, habido;   *195*
gloria del mar, honor de su ribera.
El bello imán, el ídolo dormido,
que acero sigue, idólatra venera,
rico de cuanto el huerto ofrece pobre,
rinden las vacas y fomenta el robre.   *200*

26

El celestial humor recién cuajado
que la almendra guardó entre verde y seca,
en blanca mimbre se lo puso al lado,
y un copo, en verdes juncos, de manteca;
en breve corcho, pero bien labrado,   *205*
un rubio hijo de una encina hueca,
dulcísimo panal, a cuya cera
su néctar vinculó la primavera.

27

Caluroso, al arroyo da las manos,
y con ellas las ondas a su frente,   *210*
entre dos mirtos que, de espuma canos,
dos verdes garzas son de la corriente.
Vagas cortinas de volantes vanos
corrió Favonio lisonjeramente
a la de viento, cuando no sea cama   *215*
de frescas sombras, de menuda grama.

24
The Dog, a solar salamander dressed   *185*
In starry garb, is barking in the skies,
When, dusty-haired, with sweat that on his breast
Like humid sparks or burning diamonds lies,
Comes Acis. As he sees the lovely west
Of sunset sleep that softly seals her eyes,   *190*
The sounding crystal to his lips he raises,
And sidelong on the silent crystal gazes.

25
Acis, a shaft from Cupid's bow released,
Pride of the sea and honour of the shore,
Whom to a faun, half human and half beast,   *195*
A lovely nymph, by name Simetis, bore,
Is by his humble orchard richly blest,
His teeming kine, his fostering oak-tree's store;
And this fair magnet, sleeping idol, he
Pursues like steel, loves to idolatry.   *200*

26
Ambrosial juice, newly solidified,
Which between green and dry the almonds hold,
He lays in snow-white osiers at her side,
And butter pats in verdant rushes rolled,
And, in its case of cork-bark neatly tied,   *205*
The hollow oak-tree's progeny of gold,
Sweet comb, fettered within whose waxen cells
By spring, the fragrance of its nectar dwells.

27
Heated, he gave the stream his hands, and these
Raised to his face and brow the cooling tide,   *210*
Between two hoary-footed myrtle trees,
Like green-clad heron at the current's side.
Uncertain folds of empty draperies,
Spread by Favonius' gentle breath, supplied
A bed, if not a wind-swung hammock, made   *215*
From slender couch-grass and refreshing shade.

28
La ninfa, pues, la sonorosa plata
bullir sintió del arroyuelo apenas,
cuando, a los verdes márgenes ingrata,
segur se hizo de sus azucenas.   *220*
Huyera; mas tan frío se desata
un temor perezoso por sus venas,
que a la precisa fuga, al presto vuelo,
grillos de nieve fue, plumas de hielo.

29
Fruta en mimbres halló, leche exprimida   *225*
en juncos, miel en corcho, mas sin dueño;
si bien al dueño debe, agradecida,
su deidad culta, venerado el sueño.
A la ausencia mil veces ofrecida,
este de cortesía no pequeño   *230*
indicio la dejó—aunque estatua helada—
más discursiva y menos alterada.

30
No al Cíclope atribuye, no, la ofrenda;
no a sátiro lascivo, ni a otro feo
morador de las selvas, cuya rienda   *235*
el sueño aflija, que aflojó el deseo.
El niño dios, entonces, de la venda,
ostentación gloriosa, alto trofeo
quiere que al árbol de su madre sea
el desdén hasta allí de Galatea.   *240*

31
Entre las ramas del que más se lava
en el arroyo, mirto levantado,
carcaj de cristal hizo, si no aljaba,
su blanco pecho, de un arpón dorado.
El monstro de rigor, la fiera brava,   *245*
mira la ofrenda ya con más cuidado,
y aun siente que a su dueño sea, devoto,
confuso alcaide más, el verde soto.

28

The nymph no sooner heard an altered sound
Come from the tinkling silver than she made
Herself a scythe to mow the verdant ground
Of her own lilies with its thankless blade.   220
She would have fled, but sluggish torpor bound
Her limbs, and all her blood ran chill with dread:
What hope of quick escape of hasty flight
With snowbound feet and wings that freeze with fright?

29

Ownerless fruit, butter and honey stored   225
In osier, reeds and cork she sees, and knows
With pleasure that the owner who adored
Her deity respected her repose;
And though by fear a thousand times implored
To hasty flight, while statue-like she froze,   230
These signs of no small courtesy combined
To ease her terrors and to soothe her mind.

30

Such gifts none of the lustful satyr train,
Nor savage dwellers in the trees could make,
Nor yet the Cyclops, for their passion's rein,   235
Strained by desire, the sight of sleep would break.
Weary of Galatea's long disdain
The little blindfold love-god wills to take
Her captive, and adorn his mother's tree
With the high spoils of glorious victory.   240

31

The loftiest myrtle boughs, whose lower part
The stream most deeply washes, Cupid seeks;
Her ivory bosom for his golden dart
A crystal sheath, if not a quiver, makes.
The stubborn monster yields, the savage heart   245
Melts at the proffered gifts, and then there wakes
The thought that still the leafy grove may cover,
A jealous guardian, this devoted lover.

(123)

32
Llamáralo, aunque muda, mas no sabe
el nombre articular que más querría;   *250*
ni lo ha visto, si bien pincel süave
lo ha bosquejado ya en su fantasía.
Al pie—no tanto ya, del temor, grave—
fía su intento; y, tímida, en la umbría
cama de campo y campo de batalla,   *255*
fingiendo sueño al cauto garzón halla.

33
El bulto vio, y, haciéndolo dormido,
librada en un pie toda sobre él pende
(urbana al sueño, bárbara al mentido
retórico silencio que no entiende):   *260*
no el ave reina, así, el fragoso nido
corona inmóvil, mientras no desciende
—rayo con plumas—al milano pollo
que la eminencia abriga de un escollo,

34
como la ninfa bella, compitiendo   *265*
con el garzón dormido en cortesía,
no sólo para, mas el dulce estruendo
del lento arroyo enmudecer querría.
A pesar luego de las ramas, viendo
colorido el bosquejo que ya había   *270*
en su imaginación Cupido hecho
con el pincel que le clavó su pecho,

35
de sitio mejorada, atenta mira,
en la disposición robusta, aquello
que, si por lo süave no la admira,   *275*
es fuerza que la admire por lo bello.
Del casi tramontado sol aspira
a los confusos rayos, su cabello;
flores su bozo es, cuyas colores,
como duerme la luz, niegan las flores.   *280*

(124)

32
She would have called, though dumb with fright, had she
Known with what eager name to fill the glade;   250
She saw him not, yet in her fantasy
A gentle brush his features had portrayed;
So to her feet, now weighed less fearfully,
Trusting, with timid step she sought the shade
Where, couched upon the ground, Love's battleground,   255
And feigning sleep, the wily youth she found.

33
She saw him, as she thought, in slumber there
And, balanced on one foot, above him bent,
Kind to his sleep, but blindly unaware
Of what this rhetoric of silence meant;   260
Motionless as the monarch of the air
Crowning his craggy nest, poised for descent,
Feathered with lightning, on the fledgling kite
Sheltered beneath some rocky mountain height,

34
Such was the lovely maiden, rivalling   265
In courtesy the sleeping youth, for she
Not only paused, but wished the gentle spring
Might hush for him its murmuring melody.
And now, in nature's fullest colouring,
Despite the shading branches, she could see   270
The sketch which, like a paint brush, Cupid's dart
Limned in her fancy when it pierced her heart.

35
Eager to gaze on him, she changes place
Until his manly looks are better seen,
Not to admire in him a gentler grace,   275
But prompted to admire his handsome mien.
In mingled hues his locks aspire to trace
The cloudy brilliance of the sunset's sheen;
Down blooms upon his cheeks, though sleep denies
That bloom the hidden daylight of his eyes.   280

(125)

36

En la rústica greña yace oculto
el áspid, del intonso prado ameno,
antes que del peinado jardín culto
en el lascivo, regalado seno:
en lo viril desata de su vulto   *285*
lo más dulce el Amor, de su veneno;
bébelo Galatea, y da otro paso
por apurarle la ponzoña al vaso.

37

Acis—aún más de aquello que dispensa
la brújula del sueño vigilante—,   *290*
alterada la ninfa esté o suspensa,
Argos es siempre atento a su semblante,
lince penetrador de lo que piensa,
ciñalo bronce o múrelo diamante:
que en sus paladïones Amor ciego,   *295*
sin romper muros, introduce fuego.

38

El sueño de sus miembros sacudido,
gallardo el joven la persona ostenta,
y al marfil luego de sus pies rendido,
el coturno besar dorado intenta.   *300*
Menos ofende el rayo prevenido,
al marinero, menos la tormenta
prevista le turbó o pronosticada:
Galatea lo diga, salteada.

39

Más agradable y menos zahareña,   *305*
al mancebo levanta venturoso,
dulce ya concediéndole y risueña,
paces no al sueño, treguas sí al reposo.
Lo cóncavo hacía de una peña
a un fresco sitïal dosel umbroso,   *310*
y verdes celosías unas hiedras,
trepando troncos y abrazando piedras.

36

The serpent lurks where some unshorn expanse
Of pleasant grass or wooded brake extends,
Rather than where contrived luxuriance
Its cultured aspect to the garden lends.
So is it with the virile countenance,   285
Where now his sweetest poison Cupid blends,
Which drinking, Galatea longs to seize
The venomed cup and drain it to the lees.

37

Acis, more watchful than the tiny space
His eyelids, feigning sleep, might seem to grant,   290
Intent as Argus, scans the maiden's face,
Now agitated and now hesitant.
Lynx-like he strives her inmost thoughts to trace,
Though girt with bronze and walled with adamant:
Blind Love, although he breaks no ramparts down,   295
Leads in the Trojan horse and fires the town.

38

His limbs, now shaken free from sleep, reveal
His youthful comeliness to fuller view;
He hastens at her marble feet to kneel
And kiss the golden buckle of her shoe.   300
As mariners, forewarned of thunder, feel
Less fear, and the predicted tempest too
Strikes with less force, proof of the contrary
Might Galatea's sudden terror be.

39

Soon, kinder and less timid, to his feet   305
She helped the daring youth, and when he rose
Bestowed upon him, smiling now and sweet,
Not peace for sleep but truce to all repose.
The fragrant coolness of a shady seat
Canopied by a hollow rock they chose,   310
Where ivy, like a verdant lattice, clung
Around the stones and from the branches hung.

40

Sobre una alfombra, que imitara en vano
el tirio sus matices (si bien era
de cuantas sedas ya hiló, gusano,   *315*
y, artífice, tejió la Primavera)
reclinados, al mirto más lozano,
una y otra lasciva, si ligera,
paloma se caló, cuyos gemidos
—trompas de amor—alteran sus oídos.   *320*

41

El ronco arrullo al joven solicita;
mas, con desvíos Galatea suaves,
a su audacia los términos limita,
y el aplauso al concento de las aves.
Entre las ondas y la fruta, imita   *325*
Acis al siempre ayuno en penas graves:
que, en tanta gloria, infierno son no breve,
fugitivo cristal, pomos de nieve.

42

No a las palomas concedió Cupido
juntar de sus dos picos los rubíes,   *330*
cuando al clavel el joven atrevido
las dos hojas le chupa carmesíes.
Cuantas produce Pafo, engendra Gnido,
negras violas, blancos alhelíes,
llueven sobre el que Amor quiere que sea   *335*
tálamo de Acis ya y de Galatea.

43

Su aliento humo, sus relinchos fuego,
si bien su freno espumas, ilustraba
las columnas Etón que erigió el griego,
do el carro de la luz sus ruedas lava,   *340*
cuando, de amor el fiero jayán ciego,
la cerviz oprimió a una roca brava,
que a la playa, de escollos no desnuda,
linterna es ciega y atalaya muda.

40

Reclined upon a carpet rivalling
The Tyrian hues for splendour, though it still
Was made from threads which, like a silkworm, Spring   *315*
Had spun, and woven with an artist's skill,
They see two doves alight on gentle wing
And, from the lustiest myrtle, in the thrill
Of passion, moaning soft laments to move
Their hearers with the clarion-call of Love.   *320*

41

The husky cooing stirs the youngster's veins,
But gently she eludes his hot desire,
Sets limits to his boldness, and restrains
All but the plaudits of the feathered choir.
Poised between fruit and flood, he feels the pains   *325*
Of Tantalus in thirst's eternal fire:
Brief heaven gives place to hell's protracted woe,
The crystal flees, the apples turn to snow.

42

Scarcely had Cupid let the doves unite
Their ruby bills before the stripling dares   *330*
With his own lips to suck the sweet delight
Which, like two crimson petals, blooms on hers.
More stocks than cover Paphos' fields with white,
More dusky violets than Cnidus bears,
Rain on the place where Love ordains to spread   *335*
Acis' and Galatea's bridal bed.

43

When Aethon, panting smoke and neighing flame,
With foaming bit, was scorching with his ray
The pillars which Alcides toiled to frame
Where Phoebus dips his chariot-wheels in spray,   *340*
Blinded by love, the savage giant came
His ponderous foot upon a cliff to lay
Which, soaring high, surveyed the rock-strewn coast,
An eyeless light, a silent sentry-post.

44
Arbitro de montañas y ribera,   *345*
aliento dio, en la cumbre de la roca,
a los albogues que agregó la cera,
el prodigioso fuelle de su boca;
la ninfa los oyó, y ser más quisiera
breve flor, hierba humilde, tierra poca,   *350*
que de su nuevo tronco vid lasciva,
muerta de amor, y de temor no viva.

45
Mas—cristalinos pámpanos sus brazos—
amor la implica, si el temor la anuda,
al infelice olmo que pedazos   *355*
la segur de los celos hará aguda.
Las cavernas en tanto, los ribazos
que ha prevenido la zampoña ruda,
el trueno de la voz fulminó luego:
¡referidlo, Piérides, os ruego!   *360*

46
'¡Oh bella Galatea, más süave
que los claveles que tronchó la aurora;
blanca más que las plumas de aquel ave
que dulce muere y en las aguas mora;
igual en pompa al pájaro que, grave,   *365*
su manto azul de tantos ojos dora
cuantas el celestial zafiro estrellas!
¡Oh tú, que en dos incluyes las más bellas!

47
'Deja las ondas, deja el rubio coro
de las hijas de Tetis, y el mar vea,   *370*
cuando niega la luz un carro de oro,
que en dos la restituye Galatea.
Pisa la arena, que en la arena adoro
cuantas el blanco pie conchas platea,
cuyo bello contacto puede hacerlas,   *375*
sin concebir rocío, parir perlas.

44

Monarch alike of mountain and of foam,   345
Upon the topmost rock he takes his stand,
And fills with breath the wax-bound organ, from
The monstrous bellows which his lips command.
The nymph, who hears, would gladly have become
A flower, a blade of grass, a grain of sand;   350
Vinelike she hugs her new-found tree-trunk tight,
Half dead from love, and scarce alive from fright.

45

Her arms like crystal tendrils, helplessly,
Tangled by love, knotted by fright, she threw
Round the unhappy elm which jealousy   355
With trenchant axe would soon to splinters hew;
Then while the caves reechoed to the sea
The warning which the barbarous bagpipe blew,
The thunder of his mighty voice was heard,
Whose strain, O Muses, help me to record.   360

46

'Fair maiden, gentler than a flower bent low
When dawn's first dewdrop on its petals lies,
With plumage whiter than the swan can show,
Who dwells upon the sea, and singing dies,
Splendid as is the peacock, for although   365
His azure mantle shines with golden eyes
Thick as the stars that stud the sapphire zone,
No two are lovelier, maiden, than your own.

47

'Forsake the waves, forsake the bright-haired choir
Of Tethys' daughters, and the waves shall learn,   370
When lit not by a car of golden fire,
That Galatea's eyes as brightly burn.
Walk on the beach, that I may there admire
How shells beneath your feet to silver turn,
From which, made fruitful by your shining tread,   375
Without conceiving dewdrops, pearls are bred.

(131)

48
'Sorda hija del mar, cuyas orejas
a mis gemidos son rocas al viento:
o dormida te hurten a mis quejas
purpúreos troncos de corales ciento,   *380*
o al disonante número de almejas
—marino, si agradable no, instrumento—
coros tejiendo estés, escucha un día
mi voz, por dulce, cuando no por mía.

49
'Pastor soy, mas tan rico de ganados,   *385*
que los valles impido más vacíos,
los cerros desparezco levantados
y los caudales seco de los ríos;
no los que, de sus ubres desatados,
o derivados de los ojos míos,   *390*
leche corren y lágrimas; que iguales
en número a mis bienes son mis males.

50
'Sudando néctar, lambicando olores,
senos que ignora aun la golosa cabra,
corchos me guardan, más que abeja flores   *395*
liba inquïeta, ingenïosa labra;
troncos me ofrecen árboles mayores,
cuyos enjambres, o el abril los abra,
o los desate el mayo, ámbar distilan
y en ruecas de oro rayos del sol hilan.   *400*

51
'Del Júpiter soy hijo, de las ondas,
aunque pastor; si tu desdén no espera
a que el monarca de esas grutas hondas,
en trono de cristal te abrace nuera,
Polifemo te llama, no te escondas;   *405*
que tanto esposo admira la ribera
cual otro no vio Febo, más robusto,
del perezoso Volga al Indo adusto.

48
'O daughter of the sea, deaf to my moans
As to the tempest's howling are the rocks,
Whether you sleep, defended from my groans,
Among the purple coral's hundred stocks,   *380*
Or weave a measure to the raucous tones
Of Triton's conch, whose grating music shocks
Our hearing, to my voice, for once, incline
Your ear, and find it sweet, though it be mine.

49
'A shepherd I, with flocks so well supplied   *385*
They hide the mountain tops, however high;
They fill the valley beds, however wide;
The largest river, when they drink, runs dry.
Not so the streams that from their udders glide,
Nor those that draw their waters from my eye—   *390*
Torrents of milk and tears, whose volume shows
My goods are matched in number by my woes.

50
'In nooks where greediest goats forbear to stray,
To every flower my hives send many a bee,
The fragrant nectar of whose petals they   *395*
Restlessly sip, liquefy skilfully.
To house my swarms, when April wakes or May
Release them for flight, the tallest tree
Offers its trunk, and threads of amber run
Like sunlight from their golden distaff spun.   *400*

51
'Though but a shepherd, he who rules the waves
Sired me, so if you wait not in your pride
Till, on his crystal throne in ocean's caves,
Neptune himself shall kiss you as my bride,
Hide not the sight that Polyphemus craves: *405*
Phoebus sees not, from Volga's sullen tide
To Indus' waters, scorched beneath his fire,
A sturdier groom than him our shores admire.

52

'Sentado, a la alta palma no perdona
su dulce fruto mi robusta mano;   *410*
en pie, sombra capaz es mi persona
de innumerables cabras el verano.
¿Qué mucho, si de nubes se corona
por igualarme la montaña en vano,
y en los cielos, desde esta roca, puedo   *415*
escribir mis desdichas con el dedo?

53

'Marítimo alciön roca eminente
sobre sus huevos coronaba, el día
que espejo de zafiro fue luciente
la playa azul, de la persona mía.   *420*
Miréme, y lucir vi un sol en mi frente,
cuando en el cielo un ojo se veía:
neutra el agua dudaba a cuál fe preste,
o al cielo humano, o al cíclope celeste.

54

'Registra en otras puertas el venado   *425*
sus años, su cabeza colmilluda
la fiera cuyo cerro levantado,
de helvecias picas es muralla aguda;
la humana suya el caminante errado
dio ya a mi cueva, de piedad desnuda,   *430*
albergue hoy, por tu causa, al peregrino,
do halló reparo, si perdió camino.

55

'En tablas dividida, rica nave
besó la playa miserablemente,
de cuantas vomitó riquezas grave,   *435*
por las bocas del Nilo el Oriente.
Yugo aquel día, y yugo bien süave,
del fiero mar a la sañuda frente
imponiéndole estaba (si no al viento
dulcísimas coyundas) mi instrumento,   *440*

52

'Seated, my mighty hand can still persuade
The loftiest palm to yield its tribute sweet;   *410*
Standing, my bulk affords an ample shade
For countless goats against the summer's heat.
No mountain, piling clouds upon its head,
Can match my stature, for although my feet
Are on this rock, my fingers, stretched on high,   *415*
Can write my amorous sorrows on the sky.

53

'The halcyon brooded on her nest one day,
Crowning a rock that overhung the sea,
While, bright and blue beneath, the ocean lay
To make a sapphire looking-glass for me.   *420*
I saw the shining sun my brows display,
When in the sky a single eye was seen:
The waters doubted if there shone on high
A heavenly Cyclops or a human sky.

54

'On other portals let the antlered deer   *425*
Display his age, or that fierce brute present
His snout and tusks, whose backbone seems to rear,
Like Switzers' pikes, a jagged battlement.
Of old his human head the wanderer
To deck my cave, by cruel compulsion, lent,   *430*
Where, for your sake, the stranger finds today
A better welcome if he goes astray.

55

'Once a tall vessel, which the waves had rent
To splinters, lamentably kissed the strand,
Big with those riches which the Orient   *435*
Spews from the mouths of Nile to every land.
While with its yoke that day my instrument,
An easy yoke indeed, strove to command
The stubborn forehead of the angry seas,
Or with still gentler chains to bind the breeze,   *440*

56

'cuando, entre globos de agua, entregar veo
a las arenas ligurina haya,
en cajas los aromas del Sabeo,
en cofres las riquezas de Cambaya:
delicias de aquel mundo, ya trofeo   *445*
de Escila, que, ostentado en nuestra playa,
lastimoso despojo fue dos días
a las que esta montaña engendra arpías.

57

'Segunda tabla a un ginovés mi gruta
de su persona fue, de su hacienda;   *450*
la una reparada, la otra enjuta,
relación del naufragio hizo horrenda.
Luciente paga de la mejor fruta
que en hierbas se recline, en hilos penda,
colmillo fue del animal que el Ganges   *455*
sufrir muros le vio, romper falanges:

58

'arco, digo, gentil, bruñida aljaba,
obras ambas de artífice prolijo,
y de Malaco rey a deidad Java
alto don, según ya mi huésped dijo.   *460*
De aquél la mano, de ésta el hombro agrava;
convencida la madre, imita al hijo:
serás a un tiempo en estos horizontes
Venus del mar, Cupido de los montes.'

59

Su horrenda voz, no su dolor interno,   *465*
cabras aquí le interrumpieron, cuantas
—vagas el pie, sacrílegas el cuerno—
a Baco se atrevieron en sus plantas.
Mas, conculcado el pámpano más tierno
viendo el fiero pastor, voces él tantas,   *470*
y tantas despidió la honda piedras,
que el muro penetraron de las hiedras.

56

'Over the sand, among the boiling spray,
I saw the doomed Ligurian timbers pour
Coffers that held the riches of Cambay,
Caskets that guarded Sheba's fragrant store:
Spoils of the Indies, now the vaunted prey   *445*
Of Scylla, and a pageant for the shore—
For two short days the piteous remnants feed
The ravenous harpies which our mountains breed.

57

'A second plank that day my grotto made
To save a sailor's person and his gold;   *450*
His treasures dried, his fainting body stayed,
The grisly story of the wreck he told.
In shining coin the finest fruit he paid
Of all that strings suspend or straws enfold—
Tusk of the monster which, on Ganges' banks,   *455*
Carries a fort and crushes armoured ranks.

58

'The handsome bow and burnished quiver were
Works of laborious skill, which once had been
Made for Malacca's king, a present rare,
My guest asserted, for a Javan queen.   *460*
That in your hand, this on your shoulder bear;
Mother and son alike in you be seen;
So may you, now the Venus of the sea,
Also the Cupid of the mountains be.'

59

Some goats, who dare to interrupt in scorn   *465*
His dreadful voice, though not his inner woe,
With heedless foot and sacrilegious horn
Assail the plot where Bacchus' tendrils grow.
But when he sees his tenderest vine-shoots torn
And tramped, the savage shepherd bellows so   *470*
And showers so many pebbles from his sling,
They pierce the ivy where the lovers cling.

60

De los nudos, con esto, más süaves,
los dulces dos amantes desatados,
por duras guijas, por espinas graves   475
solicitan el mar con pies alados:
tal, redimiendo de importunas aves
incauto meseguero sus sembrados,
de liebres dirimió copia, así, amiga,
que vario sexo unió y un surco abriga.   480

61

Viendo el fiero jayán, con paso mudo
correr al mar la fugitiva nieve
(que a tanta vista el líbico desnudo
registra el campo de su adarga breve)
y al garzón viendo, cuantas mover pudo   485
celoso trueno, antiguas hayas mueve:
tal, antes que la opaca nube rompa,
previene rayo fulminante trompa.

62

Con vïolencia desgajó infinita,
la mayor punta de la excelsa roca,   490
que al joven, sobre quien la precipita,
urna es mucha, pirámide no poca.
Con lágrimas la ninfa solicita
las deidades del mar, que Acis invoca:
concurren todas, y el peñasco duro   495
la sangre que exprimió, cristal fue puro.

63

Sus miembros lastimosamente opresos
del escollo fatal fueron apenas,
que los pies de los árboles más gruesos
calzó el líquido aljófar de sus venas.   500
Corriente plata al fin sus blancos huesos,
lamiendo flores y argentando arenas,
a Doris llega, que, con llanto pío,
yerno lo saludó, lo aclamó río.

60

Disturbed by this, in haste the youthful pair,
Loosed from the love-knot which they found so sweet,
Heedless of stones that cut or thorns that tear,   *475*
Speed to the ocean's edge on flying feet.
So the unwary hind, who thinks to scare
The pertinacious flocks that peck his wheat,
May start two amorous hares, coupled behind
A sheltering furrow, sex with sex entwined.   *480*

61

When the grim giant saw what silent haste
Her flying snowflakes made to gain the shore
(For his sharp glance could reach the Libyan waste
And scan the shields its naked warriors bore),
While Acis followed, never storm displaced   *485*
So many beech-trees as his jealous roar;
Thus thunder sounds its warning trumpet loud
Before the bolt bursts from a gloomy cloud.

62

The Cyclops, to prodigious effort stirred,
From the high cliff a massive fragment rent   *490*
Which, hurled below on Acis, soon conferred
An ample urn, and no light monument.
The ocean gods whom Acis worshipped heard
The maiden's grief, and sped with one consent
Till, where the hard rock pressed, the oozing gore   *495*
Clear as a crystal spring began to pour.

63

Scarce had the fatal boulder fallen to crush
The piteous limbs on the unyielding strand,
When, buskined in the liquid pearls that gush
Out of his veins, the tallest tree-trunks stand,   *500*
While from his bones torrents of silver rush,
Moistening the flowers and whitening the sand,
And Doris, bathed in tears, to whom they run
Receives a river while she greets a son.

IV

Notes to the Texts

Most of the allusions and conceits have been elucidated in the Introduction, and the explanations will not be repeated here. These notes confine themselves to difficulties of comprehension that may remain and to points that may need clarification in the relation of the translation to the original. For a detailed commentary on the text the reader is referred to Dámaso Alonso's indispensable *Góngora y el Polifemo*.

5 *Niebla's cloud*: The three opening stanzas dedicate the poem to the Count of Niebla, who took his name from the village near the Andalusian city of Huelva. Niebla means 'mist'. Since the pun is untranslatable directly, 'cloud' is preferable to 'mist' because it is more usual for this to be 'gilded' by the rising sun. The poet calls the Count the Sun of his estate, but implies at the same time that the dawn is dissipating the morning mist.

7 *If, watched* . . . : The sense is 'unless you are scouring'.

26 *Shod with silver*: *Argentar de plata* means 'to silver with silver'; the pleonasm is more apparent than real, for in Andalusia the verb currently meant to give a metallic sheen, and the metal had to be specified; in particular, as Pellicer's commentary (1630) noted, the phrase meant in Cordova to give shoes or boots a silvery gloss: it is thus the *foot* of the Cape that is 'silvered with silver'. Colin Smith supposes that the phrase meant to plate buckles with silver (*BHS*, xlii, 228), but the numerous examples adduced by Vilanova, indicate some kind of finish given to the leather.

33 *garniture*: This is one of the meanings of *guarnición*, and it is in this sense that Dámaso Alonso's commentary takes it. But the word also means 'garrison', and the conceit is lost if this meaning is disregarded. The stout trees which 'adorn' the cave's mouth with their thick foliage ('matted hair') and take away from the cave more light and air than does the boulder are the unkempt soldiers

guarding its entry. This interpretation was suggested by Colin Smith (*BHS*, xlii, 228). Since *greña* was a very 'unpoetical' word this might be considered another example of a humorous correspondence. See Introduction, pp. 48–9.

62 *Swarthy as fits its parent Pyrenees*: Literally, his beard is a 'swarthy son of this Pyrenee', one mountain from the range standing for the giant. The primary meaning of *adusto* is 'burnt black'. The early commentators record the old belief that the name Pyrenees derives from the Greek *pyr* (fire). Legend had it that a shepherd's bonfire had once started a conflagration that covered a whole mountain and caused the metals within it to flow out as molten streams; that is why Polyphemus's beard is a 'burning' Pyrenean torrent.

81 *Husk is the wallet*, etc.: The wallet contains, in addition to the fruits already mentioned, chestnuts, apples, and acorns, the construction in 85–7 being 'husk of that gift of the oak' (*erizo del tributo de la encina*).

95 *the deafened boats*: Cunningham had translated 'Fear wings with sail or oar the fleeing boats'. *Sordo* means both 'silent' and 'deaf'. Cunningham followed Alonso in preferring the former sense, but the latter, being more *conceptista*, is likely to be the primary one.

97 *Doris*: A goddess of the sea, daughter of Oceanus and Tethys, who married her brother Nereus; they had fifty daughters, who were the Nereids. Galatea was one of these.

109 *The Abyssinian pearl*: Literally, the Erythraean or Red-Sea pearl, purportedly the finest of all.

112 *Her shell-like ear*: Cunningham wrote 'pearly' ear. This weakens the conceit; the ear is shell-like in shape as well as in colour: Galatea's ear replaces the oyster-shell that was its original home. This interpretation was suggested by Colin Smith: 'the pearl is restored to its shell, to the Nacreous shell of Galathea's ear, the jewel being surrounded by the "setting" of her golden hair' (*BHS*, xlii, 223).

113 *amorous care*: *Cuidado* means care, but in the seventeenth century the word was used to denote the lady whom a man loved and served.

116 *lacking eyes*: The Spanish has 'without a lantern', referring to the large light on the masthead of ships. There is no justification for turning blind Cupid into a mariner on a shell. Though the Spanish states it is his own shell, the translation makes it Venus's (the shell in which, when born of the foam of the sea, she sailed to the shore), in order to make explicit the implied connexion.

117 *Glaucus*: A merman, whose breast was scaleless, but not his lower extremities. He was enamoured of the nereid Scylla; that he should woo Galatea is Góngora's addition (see Introduction, p. 78).

120 *the silver tide*: The translation weakens the double conceit of disproportion. The Spanish says: 'to induce the beautiful disdainful one to walk on fields of silver in a chariot of crystal'.

121 *Palaemon*: The sea-god into whom Melicerta was changed (*Metamorphoses*, IV, 519–42). As is the case with Glaucus, Palaemon's wooing of Galatea is Góngora's invention.

131 *an aspic to her sacred foot*: A reference to the death of Eurydice, wife of Orpheus, who died of a serpent's biting her foot as she fled from the attentions of Aristaeus.

132 *a gold apple*: Atalanta, very fleet of foot, agreed to marry the man who could outrun her in a race. None succeeded, until Hippomanes, who had been given three golden apples by Venus, threw them one by one in her path. Attracted by the sight of them, Atalanta stopped to pick each one up and lost the race.

135 *The dolphin strives in vain*, etc.: Literally: 'How the dolphin errs in pursuing on the water the deer on land'.

137 *Trinacria*: An ancient descriptive name for the triangular island of Sicily.

138 *And hides as plentifully*: Literally, 'Sicily, in all that she displays, is Pomona's orchard, and Bacchus's cup in all that she conceals.' While fruits are offered to view on the trees, wine is hidden in the cellars.

156 *The tithes and firstfruits*: The Nereids were invoked like the other deities; their altars were chiefly on the seashores, where their devotees left them offerings of milk, oil, honey, and goat's meat.

158 *horn of plenty*: The Spanish has the cornucopia in a violent hyperbaton: *de la copia . . . el cuerno*.

167–*Or . . . the breezes whistle*: The sense is that the sheep no longer hear
168 the shepherd's whistle or the crack of his sling, unless, replacing him, the breezes should whistle or the oak-twigs crack.

175–*Restore the whistles*, etc.: These two lines are enigmatic in the
176 original. The majority of commentators construe as follows: either Love must restore the whistling (i.e., recall the shepherds to their duty), or let the now useless dogs, because of their silence and slumber, accompany their masters. Cunningham's free rendering is hard to justify. The 'herds', here and in 155, are 'herdsmen'.

179–*tantos jazmines*, etc.: These two lines are also difficult to construe.
180 The early commentaries offer two interpretations: either that Galatea reclines on the grass beside the stream whereby her snow-white limbs appear to be causing the grass they cover to flower with jasmines; or that the jasmines are her reflection in the water. Alonso favours the former interpretation and Cunningham follows him. Vilanova, who considers it 'absolutely impossible to determine

the true sense of these lines', prefers the second interpretation: the snow that covers the grass becomes jasmines on the surface of the water. F. González Ollé, in an article that has as its title these two lines (*Revista de Literatura*, XVI [1959] 134-46), goes further: it is, he claims, a logical supposition that Galatea would first lie down, then drink from the stream; in which case she would have to bend over and immerse her face in it: the part of her body lying on the grass is the snow, the part immersed or reflected in the water is jasmine. The difficulty is syntactical as well as metaphorical. The lines, literally translated, read: 'Meanwhile the fleeing nymph, where a laurel conceals its trunk from the burning sun, gives to a stream as many jasmines as the grass covered by the snow of her limbs', i.e., the same quantity of jasmines as would cover the area of grass already covered by the snow. (But, without the comma, line 180 can mean: 'she gives to a stream the snow of her limbs'.) If 'gives to a stream' is taken literally, then the jasmines are different from the snow on the grass, namely her reflection in the water. On the other hand, Alonso points out that *fuente* need not necessarily mean a stream itself, it can also denote the bank beside it: Galatea 'gives to the stream' the flowers she causes to bloom on its bank. Colin Smith defends the 'reflection' interpretation as follows: 'To me at least it is clear that the poet wishes us to see Galathea's beauty reflected in the water, wishes us to see her as a part of the water. He does this by refurbishing the trite image "*carne* = *nieve*": as Galathea lies down beside the stream she "gives" her reflection to the water as it "melts" in the noonday sun. To rack one's brains about the grammar of the third line of the stanza, as the commentarists did, is to miss the splendour of the image' (*BHS*, xlii, 224). A further complication is later added when in line 220 the jasmines become lilies that are mown down, q.v.

215 *a la de viento*: Dámaso Alonso's punctuation of this line is here altered: *a la (de viento cuando no sea) cama.* The parenthesis indicates the syntax, which the hyperbaton obscures—*a la cama de viento, cuando no sea cama de frescas sombras*—but it makes it virtually impossible to speak the line meaningfully. Alonso explains that the 'bed of wind' was the *hamaca*, or hammock, of the Caribbean and South American Indians; it is still called *cama da viento* in Colombia.

218-*she made/ Herself a scythe*, etc.: Literally, 'she, ungrateful to the
220 green banks, made herself the sickle of her own lilies'. This takes up the imagery of 177-80 (q.v.) changing the jasmines into lilies; these she 'mows down' as she jumps up. The sickle makes it more natural to take the lilies as growing on the grass, but it would be even more witty to think of their reflection in the water as being

sliced by the sickle. So Colin Smith: 'when the Nymph leaves the side of the stream, she removes—as effectively as if she had mown them with a *segur*—the white lilies which were the reflection of her limbs in the water. (Such is Salcedo Coronel's interpretation; it is discussed at length by Vilanova, who does not wholly reject it; Dámaso Alonso will have none of it. To me it seems, as one of a series of water-images, eminently probable and highly poetical too.)' (*BHS*, xlii, 225.)

223 *quick escape*: Cunningham has translated *precisa fuga* in the sense suggested by Pellicer ('brevedad con que había de huir'), which the latter based on one of the meanings of the Latin *praecisus*, 'short', 'brief'. Alonso prefers the normal sense of 'necessary': she needed to flee but fear prevented her.

228 *su deidad culta*: This is not the normal sense of the adjective *culto*; it is here a Latinism, the past participle of *colere*, 'worshipped': 'she owed it to the owner of the offerings that her deity had been worshipped and her sleep respected'.

235–*for their passion's rein*, etc.; Cunningham translates what is clearly
236 the meaning of these two lines, but it is difficult to justify his translation from the reading of 236 accepted by Alonso in accordance with the majority of the MSS. A smaller group has the variant *el sueño afloja, que aflojó el deseo*. This reading, which is that of the first redaction of the poem, makes perfect sense: the rein of lust, already 'loosened' by desire, would be further loosened by the sight of the nymph asleep. *Aflija* can only be justified on the supposition that it corresponds to one of the senses of the Latin *affligere*, which could mean 'to fell, knock down' (the rein would be 'broken' by her sleep), but Alonso admits that there is no Latin sense that clearly fits.

238–*The little blindfold love-god*, etc.: Literally: 'Whereupon the blind-
240 fold child-god wills that the disdain [for men] hitherto shown by Galatea should be an illustrious display, a noble trophy, on his mother's tree.'

241 *myrtle*: This tree was sacred to Venus.

244 *sheath, if not a quiver*: Modern Spanish makes no distinction between *carcaj* and *aljaba*, nor was the distinction known to all the early commentators. Dámaso Alonso quotes Díaz de Rivas, who explains that the two different kinds of arrows, *virotes* and *saetas*, had different quivers; the first, obviously smaller, hung down the side from one shoulder, while the other was looped round the head. A *saeta* had the wedge-shaped arrowhead, while a *virote* had a simple metal point. The fact that Galatea's breast could have been either kind of quiver is, of course, totally immaterial to the sense.

Góngora incurs this tautology for reasons of euphony: to begin and end the line with the vowels *a-a*. The whole line has the kind of balanced vowel arrangement so dear to him: *a-a-e/i-a/i-o/i-o/a-a-a*.

247–*The thought*, etc.: *Sentir* here is not 'to feel, think' but 'to regret'.

249 *Alcaide* is, properly, a gaoler or the commander of a fortress; *confuso* here means 'dark' or 'tangled'; *más* can mean either 'in addition' or 'any longer' (*por más tiempo*). A literal translation would be: 'and she even regrets that the green grove should any longer be the dark guardian of [i.e., hide from her sight] the devoted owner [of these gifts]'.

259 *blindly unaware*: Cunningham translated *bárbara* as 'cruelly', which the word can of course mean by itself. Here it is usually taken in its Graeco-Latin sense of 'foreign': Galatea cannot understand Acis's speech ('rhetoric'). But Góngora is using it in contrast to *urbana*, 'cultured', 'polite', (as befits a 'city-dweller'); *bárbara* thus takes on another of its Latin senses, 'uncultured', 'uncouth', 'ignorant'. The meaning is the same but the conceit depends upon awareness of all the implications in the contrast between urbanity and barbarism; 'rhetoric' is a complicated art that city-dwellers can understand, not so the rustics.

275–*si por lo süave no ... por lo bello*: Although Acis's manly form has no
276 soft smoothness by which to attract her, she cannot fail to be attracted by his rugged handsomeness.

279–*Down blooms upon his cheeks*, etc.: Literally, 'flowers are the down
280 upon his cheeks, but since the light is sleeping, the flowers conceal their colours'. Since Acis is asleep, the sleeping light is taken by the commentators to be the closed eyes of Acis; since they do not see, the colour of his youthful beard cannot be distinguished. Pellicer adds that flowers close when deprived of light, but this is still for him the light of Acis's eyes. The former interpretation is accepted by Alonso, and Cunningham's translation is intended to convey it. It seems much more sensible, however, to take the sleeping light as being the fading day: the twilight made it difficult to discern the colour of the 'flowers'. A youthful beard as flowers is a Virgilian metaphor (*Aeneid*, VIII, 160). Vilanova gives other examples from Latin poetry.

281 *unshorn expanse*: Cunningham wrote 'unmown'. Fidelity to the terms of the conceit necessitated this change; see Introduction (p.40).

283 *contrived luxuriance*: This appropriately translates *lascivo*, which Alonso interprets as 'exquisitely cultivated'. See note to lines 317–20, and Introduction (p.40).

290 *brújula*: The peep-sight of a firearm.

296 *The Trojan horse*: Cunningham makes explicit what is implied in
Góngora's image. The Palladium was the ancient statue of Pallas
held sacred in Troy; the safety of the city depended upon its being
securely guarded. Its sack was made possible only after Diomede
and Ulysses had stolen the statue. The plural, Palladia, came to be
used of other civic talismans, but Góngora is clearly intending
paladiones to mean all Love's Trojan horses, whereby he penetrates
all defences. The early commentators, followed by Alonso, inter-
pret these lines in this way. Vilanova gives other examples in
Spanish seventeenth-century literature for *paladión* as the horse,
but there seems no justification in classical literature itself for this
transference from statue to horse.

303 *proof of the contrary*: Góngora says, 'let Galatea be proof of this', but
the wit lies in her being, in fact, proof of the contrary, since the
statement is elliptical: 'the lightning frightens sailors less if it is
foreseen [and more if it is not]; let Galatea be proof of this'.

317–*They see two doves alight*, etc.: Literally, 'two doves, amorous yet
320 light and swift, swooped down upon the most luxuriant myrtle;
their moans—trumpets of love—perturb the ears [of Acis and
Galatea]'. The *culto* word *lascivo*, which Cunningham translates 'in
the thrill of passion', had a good sense in Latin ('playful', etc.) as
well as a bad one: lasciviousness is alien to the erotic tone of
Polifemo. Pellicer explained the antithesis *lascivo/ligero* as indicat-
ing that amorous desire makes a man slow and heavy. Doves and
myrtles were both sacred to Venus. Cf. 241. *Lascivo* also occurs in
351.

323–*restrains all but the plaudits*: More properly, 'she allows no more
324 applause (or joyous manifestation) than the harmonious cooing of
the birds'.

328 *The crystal flees*: The torment of Tantalus was to be thirsty and
hungry in sight of water and apples that eluded his grasp. The
water (the fleeing crystal) is Galatea's limbs (cf. 103, 192, 243); the
apples of snow are her breasts.

329–*Scarcely had Cupid*, etc.: Literally, 'Scarcely had Cupid permitted
332 the doves to join the two rubies of their bills, than the daring youth
sucks the two crimson petals of her carnation'. The colour red,
earlier established in the poem (see Introduction, pp. 65-6) as an
image-symbol for love and passion, is what effects the correspond-
ence between bills and lips, which become one in the act of kissing.

333–*Paphos, Cnidus*: Two cities, the former in Cyprus, the latter in
334 Greece, which had famous temples of Venus. She was believed to
have been born of the sea off Paphos. Cnidus possessed the re-
nowned statue of Aphrodite by Praxiteles.

337 *Aethon*: One of the horses that drew the chariot of the Sun.

339 *The pillars which Alcides toiled to frame*: The Spanish has 'the pillars which the Greek erected'. The Pillars of Hercules (Alcides) are the two headlands on either side of the Straits of Gibraltar.

359 *The thunder of his mighty voice*: Literally, 'then the thunder of his voice flashed like lightning'.

370 *Tetis*: This name in Spanish corresponds to both Thetis, one of the Nereids, wife of Peleus and mother of Achilles, and Tethys, the greatest of the sea deities and wife of Oceanus. The latter's daughters were the Oceanides. The name Tethys was often used in classical poetry to denote the sea.

376 *Without conceiving dewdrops*: More properly, 'without dewdrops causing them to conceive'. It was believed in antiquity that at the appropriate time of the year, the oysters opened their shells and were filled with dew which impregnated them; thus pearls were produced. The touch of Galatea's feet was sufficient stimulus for them to produce their lovely offspring.

381 *disonante número de almejas*: 'Dissonant music of clams.' The early commentators discuss how this 'instrument' would have been played. Pellicer, quoted by Dámaso Alonso, stated that it was held to the mouth and blown. This misled Cunningham into calling it 'Triton's conch', but an *almeja* is a bivalve shell, not a conch. Triton is represented in art as blowing a shell; Cunningham probably introduced him in order to emphasize the musical instrument. Góngora had a greater sense of humour than his commentators: see Introduction (pp. 65–6).

390 *from my eye*: Góngora wrote 'from my eyes'. His early commentators are at pains to defend him from the charge of forgetting that the Cyclops had only one, some by saying that this is an example of the royal We (the plural standing for the singular), others on aesthetic grounds, since to have said 'the water that flows from my one eye' would have been a lapse from dignity.

406–*from Volga's sullen tide*, etc.: The contrast between the Volga and
407 the Indus is not the longest distance the sun travels across the globe, but denotes the extremes of the cold and the torrid zones. *Perezoso*, 'sluggish', is contrasted with *adusto* because for much of the year the Volga's waters are frozen for most of their course.

417–*The halcyon brooded*, etc.: The halcyon bird laid and sat on her eggs
418 only when the weather was calm ('the halcyon days'), which is why the sea could be a looking-glass. It was thought that she made her nest on the sea, or according to some on the shore; not, in any case, on a rock. Góngora has been justified on the basis of Ovid's account of the transformation of Alcyone and Ceyx. As a bird

'incubat Alcyone pendentibus aequore nidis' (*Metamorphoses*, XI, 746), which could mean that her nest was suspended above the sea, although it is naturally taken to mean floating on it.

423–*doubted if there shone on high*: Literally, 'the water was uncertain
424 which to believe', i.e., which of its two reflections was actually the sun.

428 *Like Switzers' pikes*: While the renowned Swiss pikemen are a delightful anachronism in the mouth of Polyphemus, the pikes themselves are taken from Ovid's description of the boar sent by Diana to ravage Calydon: 'his bristles stood up like lines of stiff spear-shafts' (*et setae similes rigidis hastilibus horrent* [*Metamorphoses*, VIII, 286]).

450 *a sailor's person*: Literally, 'the person of a Genoese'. Genoa and Venice were the Mediterranean trading nations which loaded at 'the mouths of the Nile' the goods sent from the Orient (435–6), before the opening of the sea-route round the Cape of Good Hope gave much of the trade to Portugal, Spain and later Holland.

453 *In shining coin*: The Spanish says that 'the shining payment' for the fruit was the ivory quiver.

457 *arco* ... *bruñida aljaba*: As already stated in the Introduction (pp. 74–5), a bow and arrow did not figure in the presents offered to Galatea by Ovid's Polyphemus. Dámaso Alonso has shown that Góngora borrows them from the *Polifemo* (1600) of the Italian poet Tomasso Stigliani.

477 *hind*: This word is used in the north of England and Scotland for a skilled farm-worker.

480 *sex with sex entwined*: The literal meaning of the Spanish is 'which difference of sex united, and one furrow shelters'.

482 *Her flying snowflakes*: Literally: 'When the fierce giant saw the fleeing snow run with silent step towards the sea . . .' Salcedo Coronel had this to say in his Commentary (1636): 'He called Galatea snow because of her whiteness and because of her cold nature, and having said fleeing, he said that she ran towards the sea, indicating both the nature of melting snow which runs, like all other rivers, towards its centre, and the nature of Galatea, for being a nymph of the sea she sought safety in its waters.'

487–*thunder sounds before the bolt*: Thunder is of course heard after the
488 lightning flash is seen. In 488 the syntax can just as easily be 'the lightning gives warning of the thunder', but it is clear that Polyphemus lets out a jealous roar (thunder) before he hurls the rock (lightning-bolt). Salcedo Coronel was aware that the flash reaches us before the sound, and added 'I don't know what compelled Don Luis to change it round'. Pellicer, however, wrote: 'the fussy have

(148)

the right to argue whether the thunder is heard before the lightning has its effect, or not; for the present I neither hold with the one nor affirm the other, reserving the discussion for another occasion'.

503– *Doris, bathed in tears*, etc.: For a discussion of these lines see
504 Introduction, pp. 77–8. Dámaso Alonso paraphrases them as follows: 'she welcomes him with compassionate weeping, because of his death, and at the same time she greets him as a son-in-law and acclaims him as a divinity since he has been transformed into a river'.

V

The Ovidian Source
(Metamorphoses XIII, 738–897*)*
Latin Text, with Translation by David West

The Ovidian Source.
David West

THE MODERN READER turning from Góngora to Ovid cannot but be struck by the frivolity of the older writer. In this extract Ovid is a stranger to seriousness, symbolism and moral significance. The basis of Ovid's poetry is joie de vivre.

His *Metamorphoses* is an epic poem in fifteen books and some 12,000 hexameter lines telling in chronological order some 250 stories each of which involves a change of form, from the creation of the world and the amours of the gods, down to changes associated with Roman heroes culminating in the apotheosis of Julius Caesar. A small part of the delight in all this lies in the ingenuity of the transitions from tale to tale as here in the thirteenth book where the monster Scylla is telling the sea nymphs how she had rejected the young men who came to woo her while she was still a maiden. 'It was easy for you,' sighed Galatea (13.740), 'but it wasn't so easy for me to shake off the Cyclops Polyphemus who fell in love with me.' Galatea was weeping as she spoke. Scylla dried her tears and prevailed upon her to tell her story, (13.750–897). After it Glaucus comes to woo Scylla, (13.906). He describes how he had caught some fish and laid them on the grass. They moved over the grass and returned to the sea. He chewed some blades of the grass and then became a sea god. Scylla now rejects his advances. Characteristically in these 200 odd lines we have this neat ring composition of four metamorphoses, Scylla, Galatea, Glaucus and Scylla again.

Metamorphoses 13.750–897 is this story of Galatea's love for Acis and his death at the hands of Galatea's unrequited lover Polyphemus. The excuse for its inclusion in the *Metamorphoses* is the transformation of Acis at the moment of death into a river. Góngora's 'Polyphemus' provides some information about Acis, in particular the ingenious ruse by which he won Galatea; but in Ovid the emphasis is always on Polyphemus. He is brutal and terrifying, but in the bulk of the story this aspect of his nature is not in evidence. The main theme is his rustic ineptitude. Ovid, a native of Sulmo, a hill town in the Abruzzi, was the metropolitan poet par excellence, a succès fou in the capital, and basking in his notoriety. In this episode of the *Metamorphoses*, the urbanized provincial makes a butt of the country bumpkin. In 763 *suorum* is derisive 'forgetting his precious flocks and caves' and the derision is sharpened by the jingle of the phrase *pecorum antrorumque suorum*: when Polyphemus falls in love and starts to take a pride in his appearance, the novelty of this is brought out by *iam* occurring four times in 764–6, and by his total lack of toilet requisites. Being a sheep-farmer and a giant and nothing of a beau, he uses a harrow to comb his hair and a sickle to trim his beard: like anyone else in love for the first time he has to practise smiling and simpering, and in default of a mirror he has to use standing water; he decides to perform a serenade; being a shepherd he uses a reed pipe, being a giant he has to have a pipe with a hundred reeds. Handel hits this nicely in his cantata 'Acis and Galatea' in the plunge at the end of the bass recitative *allargando* 'Bring me a hundred reeds of decent growth to make a pipe for my capacious mouth'. This burlesque note is not so conspicuous in Góngora. There are no harrows or sickles in Góngora. Góngora *propria persona* describes the Cyclops's 'single eye, the rival of the sun' whereas in Ovid it is Polyphemus himself who attempts to prove his own beauty by analogy with the monocularity of the sun. Similarly the sorbs and pears and quinces are praised by the narrator in Góngora's poem but in Ovid they are the delicious items in a rhapsodic catalogue delivered by their proud owner.

But Ovid is not much of a satirist. He is short of bile. The irrepressible sweetness of his nature will not be denied. Although Polyphemus's famous serenade is largely an inventory of his sheep farm and although it returns to full burlesque as he itemises his own charms (840–55), for the first 50 lines of the song the mockery is lost in delight. Polyphemus really knows about this farm. 'No lily has such lustre', says Handel's libretto, but the loving detail of the Latin goes far beyond this. According to Ovid's Polyphemus, Galatea is whiter than the leaf of the white *ligustrum*, taller than the alder, more skittish than the dainty kidling. In this comparison where Polyphemus's wish is fast fathering his thoughts, Handel's tumbling run on the flutes is a superb realisation of the Latin. And so Ovid goes on for seven more lines with a certain amount of padding and with some trite comparisons, but pleasing for the enthusiasm of the countryman for country things and in particular for the high esteem in which the farmer holds his own farm, its stock and its produce.

> There's nae mains like the Mains o Gytie
>> An I'm the Laird o Gytie.

Burlesque returns in the climax 796–7, where Galatea is compared to swan's down *cygni plumis* which is a dignified poetic comparison, and then to curdled milk, which is not; and where Polyphemus says that if she did not refuse him she would be lovelier than—and that is his crowning comparison—a well-irrigated garden. The full tide of these country pleasures rises again as he describes his commodious air-conditioned residence; as he distinguishes between his golden grapes and his purple grapes which he lovingly lays aside separately for Galatea *tibi et has seruamus et illas* (814). Every fruit-tree he has will be at her service, and he lists them; the same expertise is there to savour where he distinguishes in two echoing lines between his sheep-pens with lambs and sheep-pens with goats, and in a brilliant half-line gives the recipe for making cream cheese, no doubt thinking that Galatea would soon be a farmer's wife and helping him with this part of the work. Clearly Polyphemus is starting as he means to go on. And what greater earnest of love could there be than the wonderful catalogue of presents he offers Galatea culminating in burlesque in the pair of grizzly bears so eloquently kept to the end of the inventory. What a catch he was with all this enjoyment of life and eagerness to share it in love. And how like a woman was Galatea. Just because of trivial disadvantages like his being one-eyed and a cannibal, she preferred Acis. And in Ovid Acis is a cardboard hero, memorable only for his funk. Here Handel declines to follow Ovid. 'When beauty's the prize,' sings the tenor Acis to a flourish of trumpets, 'What mortal fears dying ?'. In Ovid 878–9, the Symaethian hero turns and runs away calling 'Help me Galatea please, help me, father and mother'.

So much for the joy in living which irradiates this piece and makes it poetry. Before turning to Ovid's joy in the manipulation of language, a digression on cream cheese.

Spenser has a catalogue of the beauties of the bride in his *Epithalamion*:

> Her goodly eyes like Saphyres shining bright,
> Her forehead yuory white,
> Her cheekes lyke apples which the sun hath rudded,
> Her lips lyke cherryes charming men to byte,
> Her brest like to a bowle of creame vncrudded,
> Her paps lyke lyllies budded,
> Her snowie necke lyke to a marble towre,
> And all her body like a pallace fayre,
> Ascending vppe with many a stately stayre,
> To honors seat and chastities sweet bowre. (171–80)

Ovid's Galatea is no match for this. She was softer than curdled milk. Whether or not Spenser appreciated the burlesque flavour of this comparison, he seems to be deliberately correcting or capping it. The bride is not soft, but her breast; it is not 'curdled' but 'uncrudded'; not 'milk', but 'cream': 'her brest like to a bowle of creame uncrudded'.

Much of Ovid's joie de vivre finds expression in jeux de mots. In 752 why did Galatea find greater pleasure in Acis than did his parents? The answer is purely verbal. Their pleasure was shared. Hers was unshared and therefore double either of theirs. The complexities of the amorous triangle are expressed in two antitheses with ellipses, *hunc ego, me Cyclops* 755, *odium Cyclopis amorne Acidis* 756. In 759–61 there are four different adjectival appendages to *ille*; the Cyclops was savage (an adjective *immitis*); terrible to the very woods (*horrendus* a gerundive in this playful reference to the rustling of leaves); he was seen by no visitor who lived to tell the tale (*visus* perfect participle passive): he was a despiser of Olympus, (*contemptor* agent noun). This parade of parts of speech is deliberate virtuosity by Ovid to give an effective build-up to the simply stated but astounding paradox that this monster knows the meaning of love, *quid sit amor sentit*. 764 is again an antithesis with ellipse, the *iam* at the beginning of each colon providing an anaphora which is continued in the next two lines, where in addition *rigidos* balances *hirsutam, pectis* . . . *Polypheme* balances *libet* . . . *tibi* . . . *recidere, rastris* balances *falce,* and *capillos* balances *barbam*. 768–9 are an example of an ascending tricolon, and at the end of this section *tutae veniunt abeuntque carinae* 769 shows how far we have come from the savage monster of 760–1 *visus ab hospite nullo inpune*. So much for the first twenty lines of our extract, and an analysis would reveal similar results throughout the piece. The Cyclops's serenade is a particularly rich field for such structural observations, because of the variation in the arrangement of comparative adjective, ablative noun of comparison, its adjective and other elements. Notice only that the complimentary comparisons extend over nine lines of which the last *et si non fugias riguo formosior horto* (797) includes a limiting clause 'if only you didn't run away from me'. The answering criticisms of Galatea cover 10 lines in which the last comparison is built up into a triple structure for the climax, including a limiting clause (your fleetness of foot) 'the thing most of all I should like to take away from you.' This is the wit of Ovid in this piece. Unlike the wit of Góngora, it is decorative, not functional or organic. Another fundamental difference is that Ovid's metaphors are few, unoriginal and unimportant to the poetry. Góngora's *Polifemo*, as we have seen, is reflective, mellifluous, abstruse, the play of imagination and the senses. Ovid is rhetorical, clear, the play of imagination and idea. It is the poetry of imagined reality, 'if . . . what then?' poetry, like so much of the *Metamorphoses*. 'If a nymph could turn into a tree what would happen to her feet?' 'If there were a love-struck, one-eyed, cannibal sheep farmer what would he do and say?'

Presumably Góngora would not have seen Ovid as we do. Góngora's Ovid would be much more like Góngora, than like our idea of Ovid.

The Latin text is from: P. Ovidius Naso, *Metamorphosen*, Volume 2, books 8–15, ed. M. Haupt, O. Korn, R. Ehwald, (1966)[5] Zürich/Dublin.

WHILE SCYLLA WAS combing Galatea's hair
Galatea told her story, with many sighs:
'At least the men who woo'd you were not savages.
You were able to reject them with impunity.
But although Nereus was my father and the sea-goddess Doris
was my mother, and I was guarded by a bevy of sisters,
I could not escape the love of the Cyclops
without breaking my heart,' and she could not speak for weeping.
Scylla consoled her and wiped her tears
with marbled hand, saying, 'Tell me, my dearest one,
the reason for your sorrow. Tell me the whole story.
I am your friend.' And the daughter of Nereus
answered in these words the daughter of Crataeis: *749*

Acis was the son of Faunus and the river nymph Symaethis,
a great delight to his father and mother,
but a greater delight to me, for he was mine alone.
He was handsome, he was in his seventeenth year
with a suggestion of down on his soft cheeks.
There was no limit to my love for him
nor to Polyphemus' love for me. Even now, if asked,
I could not say which was greater—
my love for Acis, or my loathing of the Cyclops.   *758*

O kindly Venus, what sovereign power is yours!
This savage before whom the very woods trembled,
whom no traveller ever saw and lived to tell the tale,
who sneered at great Olympus and its gods,
this monster felt the power of love. He succumbed to desire
and in his passion forgot his precious flocks and caves
and thought only of his charms and his beauty.
He combed his bristling hair with a harrow.
Proudly he pruned his grisly beard with a sickle,
and gazed and simpered at his gruesome reflection in the water.
His brutality, his murder lust, his insatiable lust for blood
were laid aside. The ships came and went unmolested.   *769*

CUI DUM PECTENDOS praebet Galatea capillos,
talibus adloquitur referens suspiria dictis:
'te tamen, o virgo, genus haut inmite virorum
expetit, utque facis, potes his inpune negare.
at mihi, cui pater est Nereus, quam caerula Doris
enixa est, quae sum turba quoque tuta sororum,
non nisi per luctus licuit Cyclopis amorem
effugere' et lacrimae vocem inpediere loquentis.
quas ubi marmoreo detersit pollice virgo
et solata deam est, 'refer, o carissima,' dixit
'neve tui causam tege (sic sum fida) doloris!'
Nereis his contra resecuta Crataeide natam est: 749

'Acis erat Fauno nymphaque Symaethide cretus
magna quidem patrisque sui matrisque voluptas,
nostra tamen maior; nam me sibi iunxerat uni.
pulcher et octonis iterum natalibus actis
signarat teneras dubia lanugine malas:
hunc ego, me Cyclops nulla cum fine petebat,
en, si quaesieris, odium Cyclopis amorne
Acidis in nobis fuerit praesentior, edam:
par utrumque fuit.   758

                    pro quanta potentia regni
est, Venus alma, tui! nempe ille inmitis et ipsis
horrendus silvis et visus ab hospite nullo
inpune et magni cum dis contemptor Olympi,
quid sit amor, sensit validaque cupidine captus
uritur oblitus pecorum antrorumque suorum.
iamque tibi formae, iamque est tibi cura placendi,
iam rigidos pectis rastris, Polypheme, capillos,
iam libet hirsutam tibi falce recidere barbam
et spectare feros in aqua et conponere vultus;
caedis amor feritasque sitisque inmensa cruoris
cessant, et tutae veniunt abeuntque carinae.   769

(159)

About this time Telemus son of Eurymus landed in Sicily.
Telemus was a prophet who had never failed to interpret an omen.
'Polyphemus' he said 'you have only that one eye
in the middle of your forehead and you will lose it
to Odysseus.' 'Wrong again you blundering oracle'
jeered Polyphemus, 'I have already lost it
to Galatea.' The prophecy was true but he ridiculed it,
and stalked off along the shore which subsided under his feet,
as he returned worn out to his dark cave.   *777*

There was a hill which projected into the sea
like a long wedge. The Cyclops climbed up there
and sat down and his flocks straggled up behind him.
He threw down at his feet the pine tree
which served as his staff but could have been a ship's mast
carrying a full head of sail. Then he took
his hundred-reeded shepherd's pipe in his hands,
and sea and whole mountains reverberated
to his pastoral strain. I was lying far away
under the shelter of a rock in the arms of my Acis,
but I heard what he sang and still remember it: *788*

'You are whiter, Galatea, than the leaf of the white privet,
flowering like the meadow, tall as the highest alder.
Crystal seems clouded set against your skin.
More playful you are than my daintiest young goat,
smoother than a shell fined down by endless rubbing of the sea,
like shade in summer, like sun in winter,
splendid as apples, statelier than the tallest plane tree,
bright as ice, sweet as a ripe grape
and—if only you didn't run away from me—
gentler than swan's down, softer than curdled milk,
lovelier than a well irrigated garden.   *797*

'You are as ungovernable, Galatea, as an unbroken ox,
hard as old oak, treacherous as the sea,
tougher than willow stakes or the white vine,
obstinate as these rocks here, violent as the river,
prouder than the peacock when he preens himself,

Telemus interea Siculam delatus ad Aetnen,
Telemus Eurymides, quem nulla fefellerat ales,
terribilem Polyphemon adit 'lumen', que 'quod unum
fronte geris media, rapiet tibi' dixit 'Ulixes'.
risit et 'o vatum stolidissime, falleris,' inquit
'altera iam rapuit'. sic frustra vera monentem
spernit et aut gradiens ingenti litora passu
degravat, aut fessus sub opaca revertitur antra.　　　777

prominet in pontum cuneatus acumine longo
collis, utrumque latus circumfluit aequoris unda:
huc ferus adscendit Cyclops mediusque resedit;
lanigerae pecudes nullo ducente secutae.
cui postquam pinus, baculi quae praebuit usum,
ante pedes posita est antemnis apta ferendis
sumptaque harundinibus conpacta est fistula centum,
senserunt toti pastoria sibila montes,
senserunt undae. latitans ego rupe meique
Acidis in gremio residens procul auribus hausi
talia dicta meis auditaque verba notavi:　　　788

'candidior folio nivei Galatea ligustri,
floridior pratis, longa procerior alno,
splendidior vitro, tenero lascivior haedo,
levior adsiduo detritis aequore conchis,
solibus hibernis, aestiva gratior umbra,
nobilior pomis, platano conspectior alta,
lucidior glacie, matura dulcior uva,
mollior et cygni plumis et lacte coacto,
et, si non fugias, riguo formosior horto:　　　797

saevior indomitis eadem Galatea iuvencis,
durior annosa quercu, fallacior undis,
lentior et salicis virgis et vitibus albis,
his inmobilior scopulis, violentior amne,
laudato pavone superbior, acrior igni,

fiercer than fire, pricklier than thistles,
vicious as a she bear with cubs,
deafer than the sea, virulent as a trampled water snake,
and—what is worst of all for me—you run
swifter than a stag driven by hounds in full cry,
swifter even than the flying of the wind.
If only you knew you'd be sorry you've run away from me,
you'd curse yourself for all this waste of life.
It's you that would be trying to hold on to me.   *809*

'I can offer you hanging caves, half a mountain of them
in the living rock. There in the height of summer
you will never feel the heat, and never will you feel the cold:
I could offer you apples weighing down their branches,
grapes like gold on the long tendrils of my vines,
and purple ones besides—we keep them both for you.
With your own hands you will pick juicy wild strawberries
growing in the woodland shade, and cornel berries
in the autumn, and plums,
not just black plums with the purple juice
but rare golden plums like new beeswax.
When you are my wife you will have all the chestnuts
and arbute berries you could wish for.
Every tree in the forest will be yours to command.   *820*

'Every animal you see is mine and there are more—
scores grazing in the valleys, scores deep in the woods,
scores penned in the caves. I couldn't tell you
how many I've got. It's a poor man that counts his stock.
Don't take my word for it, come and see for yourself.
Their udders are so full their legs can scarcely move round them.
The younger ones are kept in sheltered pens,
the little lambs in one place, the little kids in another.
There's always lovely white milk, some kept for drinking,
some jellied by liquid rennet.   *830*

'But not all the gifts I have for you will be so commonplace
and easy to come by—fawns you'll have, and hares and goats
or a pair of pigeons or their nestlings picked off the tree tops,

(162)

asperior tribulis, feta truculentior ursa,
surdior aequoribus, calcato inmitior hydro,
et, quod praecipue vellem tibi demere possem,
non tantum cervo claris latrabitus acto,
verum etiam ventis volucrique fugacior aura.
at, bene si noris, pigeat fugisse, morasque
ipsa tuas damnes et me retinere labores!   *809*

sunt mihi, pars montis, vivo pendentia saxo
antra, quibus nec sol medio sentitur in aestu
nec sentitur hiems; sunt poma gravantia ramos;
sunt auro similes longis in vitibus uvae,
sunt et purpureae: tibi et has servamus et illas.
ipsa tuis manibus silvestri nata sub umbra
mollia fraga leges, ipsa autumnalia corna
prunaque, non solum nigro liventia suco,
verum etiam generosa novasque imitantia ceras;
nec tibi castaneae me coniuge, nec tibi deerunt
arbutei fetus: omnis tibi serviet arbor.   *820*

hoc pecus omne meum est, multae quoque vallibus errant,
multas silva tegit, multae stabulantur in antris,
nec, si forte roges, possim tibi dicere, quot sint.
pauperis est numerare pecus! de laudibus harum
nil mihi credideris: praesens potes ipsa videre,
ut vix circumeant distentum cruribus uber.
sunt, fetura minor, tepidis in ovilibus agni,
sunt quoque, par aetas, aliis in ovilibus haedi.
lac mihi semper adest niveum: pars inde bibenda
servatur, partem liquefacta coagula durant.   *830*

nec tibi deliciae faciles vulgataque tantum
munera contingent, dammae leporesque caperque,
parve columbarum demptusve cacumine nidus:

I've just found in the mountains for you to play with
a pair of cubs so alike you can't tell them apart—
grizzly bear cubs. I found them and said
"We'll keep these for Galatea."   *837*

'Come, Galatea, lift up your shining head from the dark sea.
Come, do not despise our gifts. I know my own value.
I have been studying my own reflection in the water recently
and I am pleased with what I saw. Look at the size of me.
You are always talking about some god who rules in the sky,
not even he—Jupiter do you call him?—has a body like mine.
My thick hair comes well forward over commanding features
shading my shoulders like a belt of trees.
Don't hold it against me that my body has a dense covering
of stiff bristles. What is a tree without its foliage?
What is a horse without a mane veiling its golden neck?
Birds have feathers to cover them and sheep glory in their wool.
What is a man without a shaggy beard and bristles?
I have only one eye in the middle of my forehead,
but an eye like a great shield. After all, does not the great sun
look down from the sky and see the whole earth?
And how many eyes has he?
And another thing, you live in the sea, and my father
is king of the sea; this is the father-in-law I offer you,
if only you would take pity on me and listen to my supplication.
To you and you only I bow the knee. I care nothing
for Jupiter and the sky and the piercing thunderbolt.
I adore a sea nymph. Your anger is worse than the
                                  lightning flash.   *858*

'It would have been easier to endure your contempt
if you rejected everybody else. But why
do you spurn the Cyclops and fall in love with Acis?
Why do you prefer his arms to mine? He has a high opinion
of himself, and I am sorry, Galatea, that you share it.
But if I lay hands on him, I'll show him that my strength
is as immense as my physique. I'll draw the living entrails
from his body, tear off his limbs and scatter them on the fields
and on your waters. That's the only union he'll enjoy with you.

inveni geminos, qui tecum ludere possint,
inter se similes, vix ut dignoscere possis,
villosae catulos in summis montibus ursae;
inveni et dixi 'dominae servabimus istos.'   *837*

iam modo caeruleo nitidum caput exere ponto,
iam, Galatea, veni, nec munera despice nostra!
certe ego me novi liquidaeque in imagine vidi
nuper aquae, placuitque mihi mea forma videnti.
adspice, sim quantus! non est hoc corpore maior
Iuppiter in caelo (nam vos narrare soletis
nescio quem regnare Iovem), coma plurima torvos
prominet in vultus umerosque, ut lucus, obumbrat;
nec, mea quod rigidis horrent densissima saetis
corpora, turpe puta; turpis sine frondibus arbor,
turpis equus, nisi colla iubae flaventia velent;
pluma tegit volucres, ovibus sua lana decori est:
barba viros hirtaeque decent in corpore saetae!
unum est in media lumen mihi fronte, sed instar
ingentis clipei. quid? non haec omnia magnus
sol videt e caelo? soli tamen unicus orbis!
adde, quod in vestro genitor meus aequore regnat:
hunc tibi do socerum! tantum miserere precesque
supplicis exaudi! tibi enim succumbimus uni,
quique Iovem et caelum sperno et penetrabile fulmen,
Nerei, te veneror: tua fulmine saevior ira est.   *858*

atque ego contemptus essem patientior huius,
si fugeres omnes; sed cur Cyclope repulso
Acin amas praefersque meis conplexibus Acin?
ille tamen placeatque sibi placeatque licebit,
quod nollem, Galatea, tibi: modo copia detur,
sentiet esse mihi tanto pro corpore vires!
viscera viva traham divisaque membra per agros
perque tuas spargam—sic se tibi misceat!—undas.

I burn with love, and the more my passion is slighted
the more fiercely it boils. The full force of the volcano
seems to have left Etna and settled in my breast,
and you pay no attention to me.'   *869*

So ran his complaint and all in vain.
As I watched, he rose, and like a bull
looking for its cow, he could not stay still,
but rampaged through the valleys and the woods he knew so well,
until he stumbled across us—we had been thinking of other things,
'I see you' he cried 'I'll make sure that this will be
your last assignation.' His voice was what you might expect
from a Cyclops enraged. Mount Etna shuddered
at his shout. I took fright and dived into the sea.
The hero, son of Symaethis, turned and ran shouting, 'Help me,
Oh help me, mother and father. He will kill me.   [Galatea,
Take me to your kingdom.' Hot in pursuit, the Cyclops
tore a great block off the mountain and threw it.
Only the tip of it touched Acis, but it was enough
to overwhelm him completely. We did the only thing
the Fates allowed us to do, and Acis took on his mother's form.
The blood ran red from the rock, but soon the red
grew paler, then became the colour of a river in first spate,
then cleared. Where the rock had touched him, it split,
and a tall reed rose living from the fissure,
from the hollow mouth of the rock surged the sounding water,
and in one sudden miraculous moment there appeared
                                        a young man waist high
with new horns and reeds woven through them,
taller than Acis, and with a face of watery blue,
but Acis it was, turned into a river, and the river
ever since has kept that ancient name.   *897*

uror enim, laesusque exaestuat acrius ignis,
cumque suis videor translatam viribus Aetnam
pectore ferre meo nec tu, Galatea, moveris.'   *869*

talia nequiquam questus (nam cuncta videbam)
surgit et ut taurus vacca furibundus adempta
stare nequit silvaque et notis saltibus errat,
cum ferus ignaros nec quicquam tale timentes
me videt atque Acin 'video' que exclamat 'et ista
ultima sit, faciam, Veneris concordia vestrae.'
tantaque vox, quantam Cyclops iratus habere
debuit, illa fuit: clamore perhorruit Aetne.
ast ego vicino pavefacta sub aequore mergor,
terga fugae dederat conversa Symaethius heros
et 'fer opem, Galatea, precor, mihi ferte, parentes,'
dixerat 'et vestris periturum admittite regnis!'
insequitur Cyclops partemque e monte revulsam
mittit, et extremus quamvis pervenit ad illum
angulus is molis, totum tamen obruit Acin;
at nos, quod fieri solum per fata licebat,
fecimus, ut vires adsumeret Acis avitas.
puniceus de mole cruor manabat, et intra
temporis exiguum rubor evanescere coepit,
fitque color primo turbati fluminis imbre
purgaturque mora; tum moles tacta dehiscit,
vivaque per rimas proceraque surgit harundo,
osque cavum saxi sonat exsultantibus undis:
miraque res, subito media tenus exstitit alvo
incinctus iuvenis flexis nova cornua cannis,
qui, nisi quod maior, quod toto caerulus ore,
Acis erat, sed sic quoque erat tamen Acis in amnem
versus, et antiquum tenuerunt flumina nomen.'   *897*